HEALING
FOR
HATRED
ADDICTION

Remedies For Recovery

Willie James Webb

HEALING FOR HATRED ADDICTION: Remedies For Recovery
Copyright © 2024 by Willie James Webb

ISBN: 979-8-9907506-0-9 Paperback
ISBN: 979-8-9907506-1-6 Hardcover

Although every precaution has been taken to verify the accuracy of the information contained herein, the author/publisher assumes no responsibility for any errors or omissions. No liability is assumed for damages that may result from the use of information contained within.

Printed in the United States of America
Independently Published by Willie James Webb

DEDICATION

This book is dedicated to all persons and their loved ones who have been victimized and those who are currently victimized by hatred, evil, and injustice.

Rev. W.J. Webb

CONTENTS

CHAPTER 1
Introduction

The motivation to write this book about hatred and hatred addiction came about due to the growing acceleration of hatred being expressed in American society. Hatred is not new. However, the means to spread hatred and the multiplied means to express it are new. The advanced technology in communication and the advanced technology in lethal weapons, coupled with alien ideological persuasions, have raised the danger of hatred to another unparalleled level in history.

In addition to this unprecedented magnitude of escalating out-of-control hatred, the traditional moral and ethical restraints have been weakened. Moral neutrality, ethical relativity, political identity, and political correctness have silenced the vanguard of justice and righteousness and the prophetic voices of truth and freedom. Unbridled hatred is a threat to America and the world. This present brand of hatred seems to ignore patriotic respect and love for the country. It seems to demean and relegate the values of democracy and spirituality to a subordinate level.

Hatred is a serious and even lethal mental, emotional, and spiritual disorder. These are the primary components that compel the expressions of hatred. Since the expressions of hatred have demonstrated themselves to be against life and the values of life, these are the characteristics and symptoms of disorders. It is not within the province of human or divine order to injure and kill innocent life. Behavior that acts against its own best self-interest in deference to compelling reality, is a mental and spiritual disorder. Impulses and compulsions from within that compel persons to use drugs against their own best interest, are called an addiction.

The compulsive, irrational, and injurious nature of hatred manifests the symptoms and characteristics of addiction. Drug addiction is accompanied by euphoria and pleasure. Hatred addiction is also accompanied by a pathological sadistic pleasure. The pathos of hatred addiction sustains and reinforces the mental, emotional, and spiritual disorder. This illness disorder of hatred is introduced to highlight the serious nature and the prospects for treatment, healing, prevention, and elimination.

This work on hatred addiction is also written to illustrate the complementary treatment and healing aspects of science, art, and theology for hatred addiction disorders. The treatment of alcohol and drug addiction by medical and spiritual institutions is a classic example of multidisciplinary approaches to the treatment of addiction. AA (Alcoholics Anonymous) and NA (Narcotics Anonymous) illustrate the spiritual side of treatment of addiction. AA and NA acknowledge the power of God in their healing.

It is clear from a theological perspective that hatred goes against the nature and will of God. Hatred is against life and love. First John 4:16 says, "God is love." Hatred is the opposite of love. Hatred has no merits for existence. Therefore, there should not be any tolerance for the existence of hatred. Human beings have a duty to preserve and give life. Human beings have a duty to eliminate hatred and by God's grace to redeem the hater.

Through the grace of God, I have had the privilege and honor to work professionally with Juvenile Justice, Criminal Justice, Corrections, Probation and Parole, Mental Health, Substance Abuse, Drug Addiction Education, Public Theology Education, Pastoral Care and Counseling and Church Administration.

Much of the information shared in this book, is based on 50 years of teaching, public Theological, and Clinical practice. The list of professionals, coworkers, and clients is too long to enumerate. All have played a major part in this production. Thank you to my instructors, my colleagues, my clients, my fellow ministers, the public theologians, my wife, Wilma, and my daughter, Karen, who allowed me the space and time to do this work. Thanks be to God for guidance, insight, strength, and grace.

Each chapter of this book begins with enumerated scriptures to provide the spiritual theme, Biblical foundation, and universal perspective. This battle between good and evil, love and hatred, has been persistent since Adam and Eve, Cain, and Abel. This volume is intended to be a serious, urgent wake-up call to America and humanity.

Based on the volume, frequency, and magnitude of damages and death wreaked by hatred and evil, suggest that the multifaceted fortified hatred and evil is escalating at an unprecedented insidious rate. The threat of hatred addiction is more dangerous now than at any time in history.

There is hope and there is good news for the committed theological practitioners, the patriotic public servants, the God-fearing administrators of educational institutions, and the witnesses of the Gospel of Jesus Christ and all peace-loving people.

The good news is that we have love, the antidote to hatred. We have the science, art, laws, and religious ethics to defeat hatred. Hatred has declared lethal warfare against love, life, and humanity. We have no other option. Hatred must be defeated and destroyed.

The Bible has a great wealth of knowledge regarding hatred. Other books and commentaries also have substantial information about hatred and evil. Every generation since Adam and Eve has produced uncivilized, ungrateful, and inhumane behavior toward humanity. Since hatred is not a complete mystery, there is hope in overcoming its destructive nature.

Hatred goes against the nature and will of God. Hatred has no merits for existence. Hatred leads to darkness and death. Love leads to light and life. Hatred has a way of corrupting human life and corroding the values of life. Its history is as old as mankind. However, something new has developed in the 21st century that makes hatred more dangerous and unaffordable. It is the development of technology. This technology in the hands and control of hatred-addicted people is now capable of destroying billions of lives and destroying the life support systems of the bountiful earth and paradise that God has designed and poured out his blessings.

God has blessed us (humanity) with everything that we need to understand the nature of hatred and evil and get rid of hatred and evil. The Bible has the knowledge, the wisdom, the truth, the understanding the methodologies, and the resources in abundance to triumph over hatred and evil. God has provided generously and sacrificially, the gift of abundant life and even eternal life that has been demonstrated and played out on the stage of human history. Hopefully, this volume will be the incentive to embrace the gift of the way, the truth, and the life.

Hatred is a compulsive, toxic rage that seeks violent release onto the persons and values of human life. This rage is often vengeful and lethal. It is often expressed through hateful thoughts, emotional rage, ill will, and pathological passion. There is a pathological need to inflict human pain and suffering. Hatred addiction is a pathological sick spirit, will, and desire. It is mentally, emotionally, socially, culturally, and spiritually contagious. It is not limited to individuals. It infiltrates and permeates corporate groups, agencies, and institutions. Groups, agencies, and institutions can be designed and programmed to transmit the effects of human hatred. As with other contagious diseases, the epidemic of hatred addiction has the potential to get out of human control.

Ultimately, the Bible is the DSM, (the Diagnostic Statistical Manual) for Spiritual Disorder.

Willie James Webb

CHAPTER 2
Description of Hatred

The whole head is sick, and the whole heart is faint. From the sole of the foot even unto the head there is no soundness in it, but wounds, and bruises, and petrifying sores. (Isaiah 1:5-6)

The diseased have ye not strengthened, neither have ye healed that which was sick, neither have ye bound up that which was broken, neither have ye brought again that which was driven away, neither have ye sought that which was lost; but with force and with cruelty have ye ruled them. (Ezekiel 34:4)

The thief cometh not, but for to steal, and to kill, and to destroy. (John 10:10)

For the love of money is the root of all evil, which while some coveted after, they have erred from the faith, and pierced themselves through with many Sorrows. (1 Timothy 6:10)

Description of Hatred

Hatred Identity and Mode of Operation

Hatred is based on pathological cruelty and evil. It is a self-deceptive rebellion against human survival values. It is against love, truth, goodness, righteousness, justice, and beauty. It is defiance and rebellion against God. The hatred addicted is on a homicidal and suicidal mission. The hateful addicted loves death and hates life.

The hatred addicted takes pleasure in vilifying and demonizing the innocent. It seeks to disrespect, disregard, and destroy human dignity and human life. It comes as a pretender to deceive; a thief to steal; a robber to take; a mocker to humiliate and a murderer to kill and destroy. It is not a mental illness. Hatred addiction is an evil-possessed mind and a hijacked brain to destroy life and rebel against God.

The hatred-addicted person or persons must target persons, groups, or other symbolic personifications to unleash this inferno of hatred and evil. Some targets are chosen randomly. Some targets are chosen selectively. The targets for victimization can be based on race, religion, sectarianism, cults, political ideologies, and countless other personal dislikes.

There is a long list of justifications and rationales for the expressions of hatred and evil. These rationales and justifications for committing evil do not have to exist in reality. They can be created by the sick spirit and mind. Some of the classic triggers of hatred are jealousy, envy, anger, rage, fear, blame, shame, greed, delusions, and heathenism. This represents people who are disconnected from God and alienated from civilization.

Hatred and hatred addiction are grave threats and dangers to civilization because of the innumerable ways and methods they can be expressed. They can be expressed through hostile rhetoric, abusive threats, criminal activity against persons, personal property, civil and human rights and community agencies, institutions, and government bureaucracies. It can range from a threatening word to a nuclear missile.

The goals and the mission of the hater are to demonize, demoralize, dehumanize, terrorize, and destroy. What does this accomplish for the hater? The brief pay off for the hater is, a vain undue egotistical self-exaltation, a pathological satisfaction, and an artificial psychological euphoric exhilaration.

Hatred is unmistakably known for the damage and suffering it inflicts on human life and the world. No sane or sober mind can deny the endless list of the horrific damages hatred has and continues to wreak upon humanity. The expressions of hatred range from mean-spirited looks and gestures to an expanding array of explosive lethal violence and evil conspiracies.

Hatred is real. It has real toxic pathological consequences that infect, damage, corrupts, and destroy human life and civilized values. Hatred manifests in mental and spiritual disorders. It is often irrational, illogical, and irreverent. Hatred often exhibits criminal, homicidal, and suicidal tendencies as well as actions. The terminology, "hatred addiction," connects hatred to mental disorders and illness. As hatred is described, it becomes apparent that it is a mental and spiritual disorder. This description of hatred addiction as being a mental disorder is not for stigmatization or condemnation. The purpose is to describe a destructive human disorder so that corrective solutions can be found and implemented.

It is important to add a perspective to hatred that differentiates it from a mental or spiritual disorder. That perspective is known as "righteous indignation." Righteous indignation is an anger against unrighteousness, evil, and injustice. Righteous indignation is justified anger. It does not become damaging or destructive hatred. Justified anger seeks to correct the problem or injustice rationally and ethically through responsible and constructive behavior. Jesus Christ said on one occasion that he came, "not to condemn the world, but to save it."

The public theologian uses the energy and the outrage to do something positive and good to overcome and prevent evil through art, science, law, and theology that is derived from righteous indignation. A healthy sense of righteous indignation becomes a transforming agent to change negativity into positivity. It transforms what is real into what ought to be the ideal.

Getting back to the pathology of hatred, it must be realized that the description of hatred is unlimited in its potential for human destructiveness. It means that a sick irresponsible control of emotion or spirit takes control of a mind to do evil. The more educated the evil seized mind, the more capability of human damage. The educated, out-of-control autonomous mind of hatred is the most dangerous and threatening thing in the world. It has the potential for creating and escalating hatred and evil. It has the potential for genocidal, homicidal, and suicidal missions of destruction.

Hatred is the compulsive override of reality and truth for a negative sensation of emotional satisfaction and mental vengeance. Hatred feeds on evil thoughts, evil deeds, and evil perceptions. Hatred causes the neurotransmitters of the brain to defy reality and truth and create unreality and delusions. W.I. Thomas, an American sociologist, in his description of, "the definition of the situation," stated that when individuals define a situation as being real, although it is false in fact, Thomas says, "It is real in its consequences."

Shakespeare portrayed this reality in his tragedy, Othello. Othello was led to believe by Iago that Othello's wife had been unfaithful to another man. Othello, in a hateful jealous rage brutally killed his innocent wife. Hatred can override rationality, objectivity, and truth; and commit irreversible harm. Who was to blame for the death of Desdemona, Othello's wife? Was it the deceiver, Iago, or the killer, Othello? This question is raised to highlight the significance of rational thought, emotional control, and respect for the sacredness of human life.

The murderous act of Othello was insane, criminal, and unjustified. Serious attention must be given to the conditions and circumstances that can trigger irrationality, insanity, and murder. Jealousy can create a rage that ignites hatred. Hatred impairs the functioning of the brain and the judgment of the mind. It negates love and embitters the spirit.

Hatred is driven and motivated by evil thinking and disparaging perceptions toward another person or symbolic personification. It has a desire and compulsion to do harm, cause misery, and even destroy that which is perceived to be undesirable or non-compliant according to self-centered wishes.

Hatred, when taken to its extreme is a form of pathological insanity. This distinguishes it from regular mental disorders as listed in the DSM of the American Psychiatric Association. Regular clients of mental illness do not pose the dangers of pathological haters. The pathological haters become fixated or obsessed with harming others without rational or reality-based reasons. They are capable of creating their reality to justify their own created motivations. This extreme malevolent hatred does not regard the innocence or the humanity of others. It is consumed with its vengeful feelings, evil wishes, and harmful desires frequently against strangers and other unsuspecting innocent victims.

Hatred is possessed of an ill spirit, not just an ill mind. This ill ideological spirit seeks to express desires to hurt, humiliate, maim, and destroy the object of this emotional, psychologically venomous spirit. It is an artificially induced drive or propensity to inject projectiles of hurt and damage against life. All credible evidence suggests that hatred is not innate or genetic. It is learned and conditioned behavior and feelings from the outside environment. The influences that produce hatred are initially external to the person who harbors hatred.

A Force Against Life

Hatred is a force against life. It is self-destructive as well as destructive towards others. It is sadistically homicidal and masochistically suicidal. It progresses ultimately to the destruction of others and self. The desire to hate and kill is stronger than the desire to live and love. Hatred describes a severe case of pathological self-deception that is disconnected from the world of recognized normal reality. It is a falsely created imaginary reality that supplies an irrational justification to express hatred and death.

Hatred negates human survival values and life itself. It is the expression of evil. It inflicts pain, suffering, and the destruction of life. It is the unleashing of resentment, rebellion, anger, rage, evil, injustice, and other ill will against the interest of humanity, civilization, and life itself. It is defiance and rebellion against God. It criticizes, demonizes, and victimizes.

Corrupts Social Systems

Individual hatred infiltrates and contaminates social systems, community organizations, and cultural institutions. It is obvious that hatred has the potential to corrupt, and self-destruct a whole society and nation.

The spirit of hatred is capable of incorporating unsound doctrines, unjust policies, procedures, regulations, and laws. Unsound doctrines and unjust laws create unfair executive, legislative and judicial administrations that hurt the lives of people. When hatred is built into systems of government administration that systematically violates the constitution, human rights, and Civil Rights, it is more difficult to identify, isolate and change. Individual hatred can be more easily identified and challenged. However, systemic incorporated and institutionalized hatred presents a more difficult challenge.

When systems, in conjunction with technological intelligence, are programmed to discriminately violate, discriminate, defraud, allocate, calculate, dictate and electronically converse, how can hatred be addressed to electronic roboticized inanimate mechanisms? How do individuals defend against defraudulent, untrue, defamatory autonomous electronic messages? This is a description of the contagion of hatred in social systems and even in electronic mechanisms. Both are used to express hatred against human life.

The Gall of Hatred

The book of Deuteronomy 29:18, describes a root that bears gall. Gall is a bitterness that comes from the root of hatred. Psalm 69:21, talks about the distastefulness of gall for meat. Disobedience and rebellion to God brought about drinking water of gall to Israel (Jeremiah 9:15). The prophet Amos lamented to Israel (Amos 6:13) that they had turned judgment into gall. The Bible teaches that hatred produces bitterness as food and water laced with gall. Nourishing food and refreshing water should not be bitter and distasteful as gall. Food ought to be tasteful and delicious. Water ought to be pure and refreshing.

This out of place alien hatred is emphasized during the Crucifixion of Jesus. When Jesus spoke from the cross, "I thirst," they gave him vinegar to drink mingled with gall (Matthew 27:34). This heartless treatment of mockery and hatred against a person dying on a cross, who happens to be Jesus Christ, ought to make us lament in guilt, repentance, and sorrow. It ought to give us resolve to declare a holy war against hatred. This resolution against hatred must not relent until it is destroyed forever.

Subtle Nonviolent Hatred

A lot of hatred takes place without the appearance of physical violence. Invisible or nonphysical hatred is doing much more damage than the visible violent hatred. When crime statistics are analyzed there is an astronomical amount of physical violence. When the excessive numbers of robberies, rapes, assaults, homicides, suicides and other physical altercations take place in the American society, it is mind boggling. Thousands upon thousands of people, especially in the urban cities, are being victimized by violence every day. The numerous animosities and hostilities in the homes, the schools, businesses, and communities would be too difficult to calculate.

Hatred causes human suffering. Human suffering can be caused by judicial and administrative decisions and actions that do not require physical presence or contacts. Public policies and laws can be written and designed to favor or disfavor certain classes or certain groups of people. The public policies and laws can be administered in arbitrary and discriminatory ways. This takes the blame away from the individual and transfers it to the law or the company or the institution or the government.

When individuals are damaged by these corporate institutionalized unjust laws and policies, they have the unjust burdensome responsibility to put forth a challenge to correct the wrongful injustice. It is hateful to put such a burden on a law-abiding citizen who has been violated and wants the God given entitlement of individual and social justice.

It happens all too frequently in government organizations, where a government personnel violates the human and Civil Rights of a subordinate government employee; and that violated employee must sue the entire government organization in the pursuit of legal justice. The individual government personnel who committed the violation is immune to the suit or the liability is shifted to the government agency, itself. Assuming that both individuals, the violator and the violated, are both taxpaying U.S. citizens; what is the justification for favoring the violator and shielding the violator from being sued and from being liable as opposed to the violated person?

This is not equal justice. The imbalance is flagrant and significant. The imbalance of one individual having the sole authority to terminate or discipline another employee in government service and not be held directly accountable for suit is not justice. Additionally, it is not justice to terminate employment benefits before due process takes place. It is not justice to require the violated individual to bear personal expenses to litigate against the government that he or she financially supports. This subjects the violated individual to pay for litigation against him or herself. On its face, this is fundamental unfairness and unjust.

Additionally, another aspect of nonphysical hatred is the indefinite delays of hearings and litigation desperately needed to bring about resolution, disposition, and closure. It is hatred to delay the process of justice. Justice delayed is justice denied. Justice delayed is compounded injustice. It is not unusual at all for Civil Rights cases under Title VII of the 1964 Civil Rights Act to languish for years with EEOC, Department of Justice and the Judicial System.

The infiltration of hatred into the policies, procedures and administration of the judicial system and the Department of Justice is a most unfortunate and tragic thing for the Nation. Such administrative and judicial hatred increases the breeding ground for additional hatred. Hatred feeds on hatred and reinforces hatred.

The Love of Money

The truth of the Biblical statement that the "love of money is the root of all evil," (1 Timothy 6:10) is becoming more real every day. When one considers the ongoing cost of taxes, insurance, fees and other expenses to survive, maintain and sustain the God gift of life the dispensation of money is at the core.

It is difficult to achieve and maintain financial stability when everything is demanding your financial resources. Even when you pay the final note on your home or other real property, you must continue to pay the taxes, insurance and ongoing maintenance with more and more money.

You must pay your electric, gas, water, sewage disposal and trash disposal bills. You must pay for your electronic and communication devices. All of these prices can be arbitrarily manipulated by the providers. A long list of other fees and charges are added on at the discretion of the providers. These are examples of systemic hatred with the love of money at the root. This is legalized hatred that imposes unfairness in too many instances, of monetary burdens and suffering on disadvantaged poor people. It is hateful to take away the tools and the opportunity from any people who must be gainfully employed to make a living.

On the illegal and criminal side, the love of money causes people to cheat, steal, defraud, rob, kill, burglarize, and embezzle. The love of money and hatred have a close connection. They both derive benefits and satisfactions at the expense of others. They both motivate sick, criminal, out of control and evil behavior.

Money within itself is not evil. Money can be used to do good and noble things. It is the idolatry and love of money that is evil. Rich people can be blessings and should be blessings for the poor people. Jesus invited himself to the home of Zacchaeus, a rich man (Luke 19:1-10). Jesus did not criticize Zacchaeus for being a rich man. Jesus became a guest at the home of Zacchaeus, and as a result of his visit, Zacchaeus became a blessing for the poor. Zacchaeus said unto Jesus, "Behold, Lord, the half of my goods I give to the poor; and if I have taken anything from any man by false accusation, I restore him fourfold." Jesus complimented Zacchaeus and told him that salvation had visited his house.

Camouflaged Hatred

Hatred can conceal itself in various disguises that do not appear harmful on the surface. However, beyond the cloaks and disguises, there is pain, suffering and sinful negligence. To illustrate this further, Jesus tells the story about a man who fell among thieves, (Luke 10:30-37) was robbed and left half dead. A Levite and a priest passed by the victimized man and refused to get involved. However, a Samaritan came along and came to the rescue of the wounded man. The Samaritan proved to be the good neighbor and saved the man's life.

Is the Levite and priest exonerated from responsibility for failing to help the victimized man on the Jericho Road? Many reasons can be given, and many excuses made as to why they did not help. Two things are apparent. They did not care enough to help. Providing the needed help was not a top priority. Jesus shares in Luke 16:19-25 that a certain rich man lived sumptuously every day and there was a certain beggar, named Lazarus laid at the rich man's gate full of sores, licked by dogs. Lazarus desired the crumbs that fell from the rich man's table. It came to pass that the beggar died and was comforted in the bosom of Abraham. The rich man died and was in torment. The rich man requested in hell that Abraham send Lazarus to get water to cool his tongue.

This story suggests that there is life in hell and heaven after death. Lazarus in the afterlife was comforted. The rich man's wealth cannot help him in the afterlife. He was tormented in hell. This story suggests that your earthly wealth is not transferable to the afterlife. And the generous people in heaven cannot help the people in hell because of a gulf that separates them. Be generous in this life.

This story of the rich man and Lazarus reveals that the opportunity to share with the poor and needy is limited to the earth realm during our life time. The life we live on earth provides significant opportunities and responsibilities to share the best of human life with other human beings. We must be ever aware of the urgency because of limited time and resources.

Matthew 25:14-29 explains how three servants were given talents. One was given five talents; another two talents and the third servant was given one talent. The first servant used his five talents and gained five. The second used his two talents and gained two. However, the third servant hid his one talent. When their Lord returned, he praised and rewarded the servant who received five talents and gained five. Likewise, he praised and rewarded the servant with two talents and gained two talents. However, the servant who failed to use his one talent was criticized and called slothful and wicked and took from him the one talent and gave it to the servant with ten talents.

On the surface it does not appear that the servant who did not use his one talent did anything wrong that would deserve such harsh criticism and penalty. A closer observation reveals that God gives talents and gifts to be used for self and others. And the more the gifts are used, the more they multiply. The failure or refusal to use God's talents and gifts, camouflages hatred and rebellion against God.

God gives us talents and resources to give drink to the thirsty, food to the hungry, clothes for the naked, shelter for the homeless, visitation for the sick and imprisoned, livelihood for the impoverished, education for the unlearned and the way of truth and salvation for the lost. The Lord says, "Inasmuch as you have done it unto one of the least of these my brethren, you have done it unto me (Matthew 25:40).

Hatred is not always open and violent. Hatred and wickedness can also be passive, slothful, and negligent. Individual, economic, and social salvation are dependent upon the development and the use of the talents that God gives humanity. The neglect of the proper rearing and education of children is an extreme form of hatred. It is extreme hatred because without proper rearing and education of children, they perish and also imperil civilization. Camouflaged hatred reveals the pathology of hatred addiction. Selfishness and self-centeredness are forms of hatred and hatred addiction.

Pervasive Forms of Hatred

Hatred crosses all racial, ethnic, and tribal lines. Moses learned this in Egypt when he went out and looked on the burdens of his brothers, the Hebrews, who were in bondage (Exodus 2:11-14). The first day he saw an Egyptian smiting a Hebrew. Moses tried solving the problem by killing the Egyptian and hiding the body in the sand.

When Moses went out the second day, he saw a Hebrew smiting another Hebrew. Moses attempted to intervene as a reasonable peace maker. Moses learned that his efforts to make peace between his brothers was not only not appreciated, but one of the Hebrews revealed to Moses that he witnessed Moses killing and hiding the body of the Egyptian in the sand.

Moses became fearful for his own safety. His sincere efforts to help his brothers, were not only rebuffed with hostility, but Moses' security is now threatened. Moses fled from Egypt to save himself. This experience of Moses attempt to be helpful indicates that solutions to the problems of hatred, injustice and crime are not simple. They are intricately involved and complex. They are not isolated. There are many ethnic, social, political, economic, religious, psychological, and spiritual components to the problems of hatred.

When considering solutions to the problems of hatred, crime, and injustice, they must be approached with utmost concern and optimum priority. The solutions of hatred and crime goes far beyond police and the criminal justice system.

A solution to these problems will require a team of competent professionals representing the medical profession, social science, judicial justice, and theology.

Hatred defies simplistic answers and solutions. People express hatred outside of their particular group. People express hatred within their own groups and families. People hate members of their own household. The homicide of Black-on-Black crime in Chicago is excessively high. Crime rates in urban areas generally are higher than suburban areas. Hatred has no off limits.

No individual and no group is immune from hatred, injustice and crime. The urgency to eliminate hatred is an escalating priority because human society is interdependent and one individual's capacity for harm and destruction has increased astronomically through technology. People are more exposed to the danger from each other and in greater numbers through technological capabilities than ever before.

In simple societies and communities basic needs were provided by people who knew each other. You knew who to trust and not to trust. Generally, people knew about the sources of their water supply, food supply, the local banks, businesses and suppliers of personal services and goods. Many of the people that you did business with in the simpler communities, were known personally or known by acquaintances. The simpler societies allowed for more knowledge and more intimacy with the people one dealt with. The more you know about your associates, the lesser the need for trust in them. Strangers in these communities were rare.

The drastic change to the complex heterogeneous, pluralistic, culturally diverse and technological society presents a grave human dilemma of monumental proportion. That unprecedented dilemma is this: The complex society forces members of the society to trust strangers that they don't know and most of the time cannot see; along with nonhuman robotic automations, with personal information, basic personal needs and personal life, itself.

The grave dilemma is exacerbated by the fact that morality lags behind technology. Members of society are compelled to trust strangers and strange instruments at a time when trustworthiness is declining, and greed is increasing. Ethical values and sound doctrines are being corroded and ignored. The culture crisis is deepening. Hatred is getting out of control.

In a society where hiding places are exposed, locations are accessible, targets are visible and reachable; hatred must be eliminated. Hatred has put all humanity at great risk. When individuals and groups work against hatred addiction, they are working to save themselves and humanity.

The God given artistic sensibilities of human beings, are capable of identifying and describing hatred. Hatred cannot be harmonized or synchronized with human life. It stands out as alien or something that does not belong with human life. Hatred is the opposite of love and incompatible with human life and human values. God's gifts of science, art, law and theology can exterminate hatred and the breeding grounds for hatred.

The toxic nature and toxic description of hatred provide the clues for the antidotal remedy for the illness. The antidote for hatred is love. The antidote for ignorance is knowledge. The antidote for evil is goodness. The antidote for disease is the antitoxins of healthy remedies, cures, and prescriptions.

There are cures, remedies, and prescriptions for hatred addictions. However, persons with the disease are often in denial and resist the healing prescriptions. Self-deception is a symptom of addictive diseases. Therefore, dishonest denials can be a barrier for treatment and healing. Addictive diseases involves the brain, the mind and will of the addicted person. The damaged brain, the distorted mind and self centered will present a serious challenge for healing and recovery.

CHAPTER 3

The Roots of Hatred

Biblical Foundations

The earth also is defiled under the inhabitants thereof; because they have transgressed the laws, changed the ordinance, broken the everlasting covenant. (Isaiah 24:5)

Because that, when they knew God, they glorified him not as God, neither were thankful; but became vain in their imaginations, and their foolish heart was darkened. Professing themselves to be wise, they became fools. (Romans 1:21-22)

Being filled with all unrighteousness, fornication, wickedness, covetousness, maliciousness; full of envy, murder, debate, deceit, malignity; whisperers, backbiters, haters of God, despiteful, proud, boasters, inventers of evil things, disobedient to parents, without understanding, covenant breakers, without natural affection, implacable, unmerciful. (Romans 1:29-31)

If the world hate you, know ye that it hated me before it hated you. (John 15:18)

But he that sinneth against me wrongeth his own soul. All they that hate me love death. (Proverbs 8:36)

The Roots of Hatred

Disobedience, Jealousy, and Envy

The root of hatred has a long history. The biblical evidence indicates that hatred started before recorded history. It started in the Garden of Eden when Eve and Adam disobeyed God (Genesis 2:17) and ate from the forbidden tree (Genesis 3:6). Rebellion and disobedience to God translates into disrespect for God. Disrespect is a form of hatred. The first man and the first woman manifested hatred of their own autonomous free will. They knowingly disobeyed God. Disobedience to God is disregard and contempt.

The hatred escalated in one of the first two sons of Adam and Eve. Cain, the oldest son, killed his younger brother, Abel. Abel was a keeper of sheep. Cain was a tiller of the ground (Genesis 4:2). In process of time Cain brought of the fruit of the ground to the Lord as an offering. Abel also brought of the firstlings of his flock as an offering to the Lord as well (Genesis 4:4). The Lord had not respect for Cain's offering and Cain became wroth with dissatisfied countenance because the Lord had respect for Abel's offering. Cain ended up slaying his brother, Abel.

The first murder or homicide of the Bible was a manifestation of hatred associated with envy and jealousy of one brother against another (Genesis 4:8). Although Adam and Eve displayed hatred in violating God's explicit commandment, they did not display any animosity toward each other. However, Cain killed Abel based on a favor of God towards Abel. Therefore, it was no fault of Abel that the Lord favored his offering instead of Cain's. Therefore, this hatred and killing of Abel was unjustified. It did not make rational or ethical sense. It was God's favor. God even told Cain that if he did well, his offering would also be respected. However, there is a pathology about hatred that negates patience and other more civil and ethical options.

The Bible has many classic cases of hatred. Rebekah and her son Jacob deceived Isaac and took the blessing from Esau, the twin brother of Jacob who was rightfully entitled to the blessing (Genesis 27:6-17).

Joseph's older brothers mistreated and sold him to the Ishmaelites for twenty pieces of silver where he, Joseph, ended up in enslavement and prison in Egypt (Genesis 37:28). The Egyptians enslaved the Hebrews "And they made their lives bitter with hard bondage—and made them serve with rigor." (Exodus 1:14)

Samson was deceived by Delilah (Judges 16:17) and "the Philistines took him, and put out his eyes, and brought him down to Gaza, and bound him with fetters of brass, and he did grind in the prison house (Judges 16:21)."

Saul was jealous of David because David was a great warrior who also killed Goliath, the Philistine giant. When Saul heard the women singing and dancing saying, "Saul has slain his thousands, and David his ten thousands," (1 Samuel 18:7-8) and this comparison made Saul wroth, and he began a pursuit to kill David.

The culmination of hatred toward Jesus was so severe that the crowd chose a known criminal to be released instead of Jesus. When Pilate asked, "What shall I do then with Jesus which is called Christ?" (Matthew 27:22) They all say unto him, "Let him be crucified." Disobedience, jealousy, and envy put Jesus on the cross.

Agencies of Hatred Elimination

In spite of the long well-known history of the hatred of disobedience, jealousy, and envy; no serious focus has been set forth to eliminate hatred. America ended slavery in 1865. It ended legal racial segregation in 1964. America has ended many disease epidemics through the Center for Disease Control. It has reduced unsafe food, drugs and beverages through the Food and Drug Administration. It has reduced environmental health hazards through the Environmental Protection Agency. America has reduced unsafe working conditions through OSHA (Office of Safety and Health Administration). America has instituted a long list of legislation and agencies to protect and safeguard human life. Commendations are in order for the protection and safeguards for human life and wellness. All these protections for human life must remain and be enhanced. However, the insidiousness of the growing victimization and lethality of hatred requires a new focus and specialized agencies to eliminate this menacing threat to civilization.

The diminution and elimination of hatred requires an agency that can treat the whole person for the whole health for the whole world. The doctrines used must be sound with principles that are universally valid. The approach and methodology must take into consideration the new component that increases exponentially, the damage of hatred. That new component is technology. The specialized hatred elimination agency must be skilled and accomplished in the understanding of spiritual, intellectual and ideological ethics. Technology developed and driven by faulty ideologies are extremely dangerous. In a global, culturally diverse, religiously pluralistic, and heterogeneous world, there are only a few agencies that are capable of establishing a global moral compass and methodology capable of eliminating hatred.

The good news is that there is sufficient relevant knowledge, plans, methodologies, and agencies to eliminate hatred. The malady and epidemic of hatred is escalating. Now is the time to focus on eliminating the number one enemy to humanity.

Hatred Destroys - Not Weapons

Hatred and the means of expressing the violence are not the same. Hatred is the evil will, desire and intention to hurt, damage and destroy life. Some of the means used to hurt, damage and destroy life and the values of life are guns, bombs, knives, stones, motor vehicles and other tools that serve the destructive hateful purpose. The weapons and tools of violence are not the hatred or the evil.

Invariably, when violent crimes are committed by guns, there is an outcry to ban guns, restrict access to guns and outlaw guns. It is amazing that the bulk of the criticism goes against guns. The guns do not kill and commit crimes. Guns are often used to commit murder and other crimes. No gun has ever been convicted in court or sentenced to serve time in prison. Guns and tools do not commit crimes. Why not blame the hatred and evil? Why not blame the human tolerance for hatred and our negligence for the breeding grounds for hatred?

Hatred is Learned after Birth

There are a variety of things and conditions that feed into the roots of hatred. It has been established that children are not born with hatred. Hatred is learned, conditioned, and influenced from the outside world and that which is external to the child's psychic world. The learning and conditioning process begins when the child is born.

The sensory perceptions of the child are activated at birth. The stimuli of light, touch, sound and odor impact on the child from the outside. The newborn infant has no concept and interpretation of the meanings of these external bombarding stimuli of light, sound, touch and odor. At this infantile stage, the child has no concept of hatred nor love. It is a human vessel ready to be taught the fundamentals of life and living, beginning at zero. This is the significant advantage that parents and societies have over their children. Parents have significant control over what their children are taught and exposed to.

The child has a long period for rearing and development for this crucial and critical preparation for life. In most societies, youth are not considered as adults until they are 18 or 21 years of age. Children go through the developmental stages of infancy, childhood, adolescence, young adult, and adulthood.

God and nature have determined this long period of years for the development and rearing of children for a reason. This long period of time for rearing, teaching, socializing, and civilizing the child provides ample opportunity to "Train up a child in the way he should go, and when he is old, it will not depart from him" (Proverbs 22:6). This background regarding the total dependence and innocence of children born into the world will be used to elaborate on the roots of human hatred.

What are the effects on the child when it is deprived of proper maternal nurturing? A helpless infant and child have a need to be held, embraced in warmth and softness. It has a need to hear the pleasant loving voice of the mother of which it was a part. Nothing can be more pleasant for a child than to be embraced and nurtured by its mother. Some children are deprived of the needed consistent maternal nurturing. Unfortunately, some children are neglected and deprived of the consistent nurturing and love of its mother. Some children are even abused by hatred when they need love.

It is conceivable that when a child is deprived, neglected, and abused, that the child experiences frustration, pain and suffering. The child begins to get messages and experiences of being in an unfriendly place. It is also conceivable that the child dislikes these experiences. It is also conceivable that the child may dislike whoever is responsible for this neglect, abuse, pain, and suffering. Unjust pain and suffering can introduce one to hatred even at a young age. Constant and consistent love and care can neutralize the roots of hatred. Love is the most effective antidote against hatred.

A lack of true personal self-identity can increase the vulnerability for hatred. When a person has not discovered their spiritual identity as a child of God, they may not know that hatred is not a proper role for them to play. When a person discovers their personal identity in God, they realize that hatred is not of God.

Therefore, it is very important that children begin a Biblical literacy program early in their childhood. Well trained Sunday School and Bible study teachers can be very helpful in providing Biblical knowledge. Biblical knowledge helps youth and all people to learn about God, hope, faith and love. Also, it teaches about the great heroes of faith. The Bible has many classic heroes of faith. These heroes of faith, inspires faithful and positive living in others. This provides insulation against the roots of hatred.

The Bible gives illustrations that God is the potter, and we are the clay, and God can make us and mold us after his way (Isaiah 64:8). That is the great advantage that parents have over their children. Responsible parental teaching can mold the child, fashion, and instill values of respect and love. The values of love and respect when sown deeply, can negate the roots of hatred.

A positive purpose for living must be provided for every child and every person. They must have something noble and significant to believe and something productive and prosperous to do. Since, "nature abhors a vacuum," when a person does not have something significant to believe, a significant purpose for living and something worthwhile to do; they are vulnerable for hatred and evil activities and purposes.

Character education must be a top priority for teaching children at home and in school. Character education minimizes the need to hate. It minimizes the waste and misuse of time, energy, and resources. The ignorance regarding the significance of good character allows a place for hatred.

A lack of normal growth and development can be an inducement to hatred. When individuals become a prisoner to childhood they often become resentful when they do not keep pace with their peers. To be stuck in childhood is to lack responsibility, discipline, and maturity. Limited intellectual competence along with emotional immaturity often results in the inability to manage resentment, anger, rage, and hatred.

Adults who have been imprisoned in childhood and perceive themselves as being inferior, unfavored and a failure; they often develop hatred. The Apostle Paul alludes to the significance of growing up when stated in (1 Corinthians 13:11): "When I was a child, I spoke as a child, I understood as a child, I thought as a child; but when I became a man, I put away childish things." It is vitally imperative for all persons to grow up beyond the incompetence, immaturity, and the irresponsibility of childhood. The goal of humanhood, is to grow up into a mature, competent, responsible loving adult. Festering hatred in an adult body with emotional immaturity and devoid of love can be a lethal combination. Growing up responsibly diminishes a breeding ground for hatred.

Codes of secrecy and codes of silence create conditions for hatred to take root and grow.

Codes of Secrecy and Silence

Certain codes of secrecy and silence breed hatred. Too often, and especially in many American institutions and agencies, wrongful policies, procedures, and practices are met with silence. Unfair and unjust laws are often ignored by leaders and administrators. Unfortunately, the code of silence is practiced by the church and clergy as well. Even if prevailing injustices are not spoken about, the silence still breeds hatred. Injustice, individually and corporately; and in all of its varied forms; is the number one breeder of hatred addiction. Fairness and justice are basic human needs.

It is common knowledge that merit system-based government allocations of resources and goods are not based on merit. They are based on subjective personal favoritism and "buddy systems." The elimination of non-merit systems in a democratic form of government is injustice. Injustice breeds hatred. The deprivation of character education and responsible discipline in public schools is injustice. The deprivation of the Biblical knowledge of God in the public schools and all educational institutions is an injustice that creates a breeding mind and a breeding ground for hatred.

There is too much silence about the knowledge of the Bible and God. There is too much silence about the Savior, Jesus Christ. There is too much silence about the improper rearing and education of children. There is too much silence about the use and abuse of alcohol and other drugs in all sectors of society.

When wrongdoings are openly practiced that violate human rights, the U.S constitution and divine laws of God, and they are met with silence, hatred and resentment are bred. When young impressionable minds witness unacknowledged and unconfronted human violations, bad examples are shown, and seeds of hatred are sown.

Thousands and millions of people are victimized on the roadside of life in America. Too often, these painful victimizations are met with silence and indifference. The story of the Good Samaritan (Luke 10:33) illustrates how upstanding people ignore the pain and suffering of people who are victimized. The story indicates that the "Levite" who had a respectable position and went passed the wounded man. Likewise, the priest, who held a religious office, walked past the wounded man on the Jericho Road.

When human suffering becomes ignored, invisible, inaudible, and unimportant, the breeding ground of hatred increases. Jesus identifies with victimized people and says, "Inasmuch as you have done it unto one of the least of these my brethren, you have done it unto me" (Matthew 25:40).

It must be recognized in this 21st century that this vast human suffering is not just benign neglect; it is criminal negligence. This breeding ground of hatred is developing alien evil ideologies with the availability of technological massive destructibility against humanity.

Eliminating the breeding grounds of hatred must be a top priority. Human beings inhabit the planet earth. The earth is very much finite. It has finite resources and finite conditions to sustain life. The increasing potential of the backlash of hatred is a real growing threat to humanity. This threat, with the help of technology can be increased to monumental proportions to the detriment of mankind.

It is comforting to know that all the credible evidence suggests that hatred is not prenatal. It does not exist in the fetus. Dr. Maria Montessori explains in her book, The Absorbent Mind, that the child at birth, "bears within him constructive possibilities, which must unfold by activity in his environment." The living body constructs itself in response to the surrounding environment. Hatred is conditioned, taught, and learned in social interaction with the outside environment.

This gives great credence to the scripture that says, "Train up a child in the way he should go and when he is old, he will not depart from it (Proverbs 22:6). The influence of the social environment and the culture are well known in the development of the human personality, attitudes, and values.

Hopeful Good News

The exploration of the roots of hatred reveals hopeful news. That hopeful news is that hatred does not have a mysterious origin. Hatred is not found in the genetics of childbirth. It is not found in the human embryo or fetus. It does not have an independent coexistence with the child.

All credible evidence regarding human hatred suggests that human hatred is conditioned and learned attitudes, values, beliefs, and behaviors from the external environment of the child. The roots of hatred can be isolated, identified, analyzed, and synthesized. The environment and conditions of hatred development can be rationally, scientifically, and theologically understood, controlled, diminished, contained, and even eliminated.

Injustice Breeds Hatred

Injustice ferments Hatred and Violence. When the established systems of justice breakdown, the victims of injustice feel that they have a right to avenge themselves. The Bible teaches that vengeance belongs to God (Romans 12:19) (Hebrews10:30). However, there are so many who do not know God or the Word of God. Being without this Biblical Knowledge, the victims of injustice feel justified in taking the law into their own hands. They often feel a "righteous indignation," and in a roughshod way they often commit violence, even against innocent people.

Therefore, it can be legitimately asserted that injustice, real or perceived, is a root cause of hatred. There are reasons for hatred. Sometimes the reasons are rational even if not justified. The injustices are clearly based on evidentiary facts in many cases. Sometimes faulty perceptions, misperceptions and distorted reality can engender hatred.

The serious efforts to eliminate injustice in society would go a long way in eliminating the growing hatred in America and the world. Psychotrauma: The Human Injustice Crisis analyzed many cases of violence traceable to perceived injustice. The number one responsibility of government leadership is to administer justice for all the people. When justice destabilization the society, hostilities, conflicts, destabilization, and wars increase. Just, righteous, informed, knowledgeable and wise leadership is critical for a just, stable, and peaceful society. If the head is sick, the whole body will be unsound and suffer (Isaiah 1:5-6).

The absence of strong just leadership causes division and chaos in the society. The book of Judges states that there was a time in Israel's history when they had no king, and "every man did that which was right in his own eyes (Judges 21:25)." A lack of just leadership breeds disorder, disunity, injustice, and hatred. Just leadership in government and in the general society is mandatory for peace and harmony in the society. When people feel that they are mistreated, they develop negative attitudes and bad feelings. These negative attitudes and bad feelings often progress to hatred.

Injustice disrupts the mental emotional and physiological equilibrium of victimized individuals. This disruption in a person's life can cause drastic changes in the person's attitude and behavior. It can cause clinical depression, social dysfunctionality, mental instability, and mental disorders to the extent of precipitating insanity, homicidal and suicidal violence.

Most Americans have not developed a consciousness of the serious impact and consequences of serious impact and consequences of injustice on a person's life. Many times, these injustices or perceived injustices traumatize and paralyze an individual's life so severely, that their only perceived defense and vindication for their human dignity, integrity, and life, is violence against those whom they feel are responsible.

This enraged hatred is sometimes turned against the victimized individual, himself. Americans, all persons, and especially the judicial justice system, must develop a consciousness of the bitter seeds and roots of injustice. Hatred and violence could often be abated and ameliorated if there were justice in the Justice System.

The connection and relationship between injustice and violence are rarely correlated. Frequently, violent acts are vengeful responses to injustice or perceived injustice. Some of such cases are documented in the book, <u>Psychotrauma-The Human Injustice Crisis</u>. When a person is enraged with hatred; sometimes they commit violence and even murder against others, even innocent people. Naturally, such persons are generally condemned. However, what most people do not understand about the traumatized mind, is that it personalizes other persons, other people, and one's own people are to blame for, "my painful undeserved predicament." "They don't care about me." "They think that they are better than I am." "I am just a nobody." "I have nothing to lose." "I don't care anymore." "Nobody cares about me." The consuming hatred and hurt catapults the victim of unrelieved injustice pain into the abysmal oblivion of death.

Injustice is the major soil for the bitter seeds of hatred and violence to grow. It is a corrosive, corruptive and pathological evil that undermines the health, stability, and life of the society. Individuals are the originators and perpetrators of injustice. However, injustice can be systemic or established in agencies, institutions, and other groups.

Systemic injustice can be incorporated in organizations and agencies by way of laws, policies, regulations, and procedures. These regulations can be designed for flexibility and subjective decision making. Subjective and arbitrary decision making are increasing in the American government and society in general. This flexible, subjective, and arbitrary administrative and bureaucratic decision-making work against the administration of justice in the society.

Merit based systems of personnel selection, contractual agreements and other allocations of government services are being diminished. There were more merit systems and more equal opportunity consciousness in the1960s than there are in 2017. There is a growing personnel selection and government administrative process based on personal favoritism, economic greed, political identity, and political correctness.

The problems of obtaining justice in the justice systems and the judicial system is compounded by the cumbersome technical legalistic procedures, conflicts of interests, unethical lawyers, unaccountable judicial discretionary judges.

Social justice, administrative justice and judicial justice must be just if it is to be credible and respected. Justice in the Department of Justice or justice in the courtroom must be based on just decisions. Arbitrary and random decisions by courts of law is not justice. Such arbitrary decisions not only mock justice, but it is additional injustice. Imagine spending a lot of money to obtain lawyers, sustaining the loss and damage of injustice and long waiting periods to get a hearing; and instead of getting justice and relief, you get injustice and insult. Such shock and disappointment can trigger traumatic hatred in the best of human beings, and it often does.

The business of justice is very, very serious. It is the balance of human equality and fairness in the allocation and distribution of goods, services, and values. Injustice is a great destabilizer. It destabilizes minds, organizations, and nations. Injustice is very damaging to the emotional and mental health of victimized individuals. According to Psychotrauma: The Human Injustice Crisis, injustice creates a deficit in the human potential.

The assurance and realization of individual, social, administrative, and judicial justice would go a long way in reducing hatred in America and the world. Individual and social justice are human rights. Justice was not meant to be bought. It was meant to be free. The classic mandate about justice was given by the Prophet Amos, "But let judgment run down as waters, and righteous as a mighty stream (Amos 5:24).

Satan did not believe that Job's faith in God was sincere. To doubt God and disavow truth is hateful. So, God allowed Job's faith in God to be tested. Job suffered and endured a variety of misfortunes in his life. Job was aware that God knew about his suffering and allowed it to happen. But Job kept his faith in God. He told God, "Though you slay me, yet will I trust you." "When I am tried, I will come forth as gold." "I will wait until my change come."

Job's undeserved suffering proved that Job was not serving God for material prosperity, neither for a good family life, neither for a good name in the community, nor for his good health. Job lost all these things. However, he kept his faith in God. The conclusion is that Job served God for nothing but his soul. He held on to his soul and his belief in God. The job was restored. Regardless to what hatred may cause you to lose, God is able to restore. God is a God of restoration. You cannot lose anything that God cannot restore.

- Egyptian Bondage
- Daniel in the Lion's Den
- Hebrew Children in Fiery Furnace
- Jesus on the Cross
- Black African American Enslavement

They and millions of others have been delivered from hatred and bondage by haters. The Balm of Gilead, the Great Physician, and the Resurrection of Jesus Christ are still in the healing and restoration business.

CHAPTER 4

Illustrations of Hatred

He is despised and rejected of men; a man of sorrows, acquainted with Grief: and we hid as it were our faces from him: he was despised, and we esteemed him not. (Isaiah 53:3)

The people sat down to eat and to drink and rose up to play. (1 Corinthians 10:7)

Pilate, therefore, willing to release Jesus, spake again to them. But they cried, saying, Crucify him, Crucify him. (Luke 23:20-21)

For I was hungered, and ye gave me no meat; I was thirsty, and ye gave me no drink: I was a stranger, and ye took me not in naked, and ye clothed me not: sick, and in prison, and you visited me not. (Matthew 25:42-43)

For they are being ignorant of God's righteousness, and going about to establish their own righteousness, have not submitted themselves unto the righteousness of God. (Romans 10:3)

Illustrations of Hatred

Ethnic Family Hatred

There are too many illustrations of hatred in the American families. Generational hatred in too many families are being passed to the children and perpetuated through successive generations. If hatred becomes the foundation of early socialization and personality development, it is most difficult to acculturate human respect and dignity as adults. It is very difficult to discard or unlearn negative attitudes and hateful behaviors that are taught and ingrained in childhood and adolescence.

Many children are exposed to the hateful and antagonistic relationships of their parents or heads of households. They (children) often witness and experience shame and blame, demeaning ridicule, hateful deceit, malicious provocations, hurtful allegations, scornful abuse, maternal and paternal neglect and deprivation of love and care. These poisonous relationships within the family create unhealthy children and relationships that spill over into the community and society.

These toxic relationships of hatred destroy the family from within. When their words are unkind, their presence despised, their silence is evil, and their absence is good riddance; these are stark illustrations of family hatred and pain.

The evidence suggests that family hatred is more prevalent among the socio-economic deprived groups and communities than the more affluent. It is necessary to provide this socio-economic deprivation when discussing hatred and violence in poor families and communities to a larger context for understanding some of the reasons for this disproportionate hatred and violence. This larger context frequently suggests a hatred of neglect, deprivation and indifference of the public officials and public policy makers. Administrative and judicial hatred at the top contributes to violent hatred at the bottom.

Maslow's Hierarchy of needs indicates a deprived mass of people who are crowded at the base of the triangle. Maslow indicates that these people at the bottom spend most of their time and energy meeting their basic and primary physiological and safety needs. These consist of food, clothing, shelter, and safety. The implication is that the bulk of the people in poverty and on the bottom are deprived of the opportunities to develop more advanced social and civilized values and cultural enrichment. This undertow of poverty and blighted living conditions hinder self-actualization and human refinement.

Children who are born of parents who happen to be at the bottom tier of Maslow's Hierarchy of needs, start life with decided disadvantages. In many instances the parents were born at the bottom of the socio-economic ladder. Many poor people, especially Black Americans, have labored with generational poverty. It is passed on from generation to generation. There are many exceptions where poor people and poor Black Americans have escaped the vicious cycle of generational poverty and have gotten into the main stream or the upper tier of Maslow's Hierarchy of Needs. Poverty remains astronomically high for many Americans, and especially for the Black Americans. The statistics are available to study the indices and the detrimental consequences of poverty in America.

Who and what is responsible for the generational persistence of poverty and the associated social ills? No single individual or agency can be identified. However, when the magnitude and longevity of poverty is considered in Biblical, Christian, democratic America; how can this systemic hatred that perpetuates such a multitude of suffering be identified?

It is not difficult to identify the specifics of the hatred of the people at the bottom. We can study and analyze dysfunctional families, school problems and failures, unemployment, blighted communities, and crime. Hatred is demonstrated in very graphic and visible ways of the people at the bottom. They do not have many shields or coverings to hide behind. Therefore, their lives and their hatred are more visible than those who are at the top of the hierarchy of privilege.

Invisible Covert Hatred

As we look for illustrations of hatred, we must not overlook the more invisible hatred that exists at the top. This hatred at the top is more invisible and difficult to see and identify. It is also much more systemic. It is not necessarily done by specific individuals. Systemic hatred is embedded in laws, or ordinances, policies, regulations, administrative procedure, executive privileges, and judicial discretions.

Another difficulty in identifying systemic hatred is because most of the individuals who direct, interpret, and administer the laws, policies, ordinances, regulations and procedures do not consider themselves as haters of humanity. They may not even realize that they are part of an organization or institution of hatred. Many are satisfied that they are good, decent, and law-abiding citizens. And yet, this unacknowledged and unrecognized systemic hatred continue to perpetuate generational poverty, human victimization, and suffering.

Tragically, the victims at the bottom get blamed for hating and victimizing each other, without being able to identify the insidious and invisible hatred inflicted upon them from the top. Public theology has the tools to examine, analyze and synthesize systemic hatred. It is critical that this analysis be done for an equitable resolution. The reason being is that hatred is so much out of control, lethal and unpredictable that everyone is threatened and at risk. Mental and spiritual disorders of this present magnitude of hatred epidemic proportion is much more dangerous than physiological diseases.

Diseases of the physical body can be more precisely isolated, treated and controlled than hatred which is a disorder of mind and spirit. Mental and spiritual disorders are disposed to use the physical body to do unpredictable actions and damages. Unidentified and uncontained hatred are the greatest threats to civilization. Hatred addiction is capable of unlimited destruction along with self-destruction. To quote Dr. Martin Luther King, Jr. "Injustice anywhere is a threat to justice everywhere." Hatred addiction is exponentially worse than injustice. Hatred is the acting out of injustice. Hatred is the practice of injustice. Hatred and injustice are intertwined evil to wreak wickedness on humanity.

Cultural and systemic corporate hatred provides a serious challenge to the practitioners of justice, righteousness, and love. Systemic injustice embedded in organizations, social systems, and cultures, is difficult to isolate, separate and extricate. Systemic hatred represents the incorporation of human ill will, ill wishes, and ill sentiments. It is incorporated hatred addiction in a human organization. Organizations and administrations of hatred cause human pain and suffering.

It is hatred addiction because it is a pathology of benefit for those who perpetuate the sick hatred system. Addiction is a harmful and destructive practice that provides pleasure and euphoric experiences that are artificially and superficially induced. Addiction is a medical and spiritual disorder. Those who receive pleasure and benefits from sick social systems, protect, defend, and perpetuate their existence. It is the addictive aspect of systemic hatred that makes it so difficult to change. The elimination of hatred addictive systems would eliminate or reduce benefits and pleasure of certain recipients and benefactors. Therefore, there is great resistance to systemic hatred addictive social systems. However, they can be changed, in spite of the self-centeredness of addictive disorders.

Public Theology

The Christian Institute of Public Theology and the Christian Association of Public Theologians have the knowledge base to bring the needed changes and transformations in individual and systemic hatred addictions. These two organizations were incorporated through the State of Georgia in 2002. They have conducted 12 successful annual conferences and many courses in theology and addiction.

Public theology utilizes for education, prevention, treatment and restoration, four areas of recognized and validated bodies of knowledge. These 4 bodies of knowledge consist of science, art, law and theology. These are foundational bodies of universal knowledge that impact on the totality of the human experience. These four bodies of knowledge encompass the whole body and total personality of the individual. Public theology is designed for the whole gospel, for the whole person and for the whole world. It utilizes the recognized body of scientific knowledge, artistic knowledge, knowledge of Law, theology and religion. Public theology has the capability to analyze and evaluate what is the existing status quo. Public theology also has the capability to propose and recommend what ought to be and what was intended to be by the creator. God has established just and righteous standards for all people. Public theology promulgates those standards.

Insidious Nature of Hatred

Hatred manifests itself in multifaceted and innumerable ways. Some of these manifestations of hatred were observed in classroom settings by an EAP (Employee Assistance Program) Specialist of Black American youth between the ages of 17 and 25 referred by the U.S. Labor Department for job training.

These classroom and group counseling symptoms of hatred are shared to provide insight into the American culture crisis of hatred. These young people were not born with these negative attitudes and anti-social dispositions. They are culturally acquired.

Additional information about troubled and at-risk American youth can be found in the publication, "New Possibilities for Juvenile Justice".

These symptoms are enumerated for future study and a serious search for remedies and solutions. The following symptoms were expressed and exhibited between 2002-2004:

1. Talking out impulsively.
2. Disregard for instructions and rules (as well as for the instructor).
3. Responsive to the most negative influences in the group settings.

4. Intolerance to silence in the group setting (manifest need for noise).
5. Expresses emotional immaturity and a lack of seriousness dictated by the instructional setting.
6. Expressions of uncivil socialization.
7. Mainstream cultural deprivation.
8. Spiritual impoverishment.
9. Deficit in personal awareness.
10. Anti-social behavior and attitude.
11. Anti knowledge, anti-education, anti-intellectual.
12. Undisciplined disposition.
13. Initiates and participates in abusive and negative influence in the group
14. Negative behavioral orientation.
15. Deficits in future orientation (lack of investment and plans for future).
16. Disregard for and a lack of a sense of priorities.
17. Disregard for ethical behavior and human considerations
18. Lack empathy and compassion
19. Acts and responds impulsively.
20. Self-imposed deafness (selectively tunes out the seriousness of the subject and or the occasion).
21. Mental flight from the light of enlightenment.
22. Spiritual retreat into darkness and ignorance.
23. Seeks delight in confusion.
24. Seems to be motivated by creating or participating in chaos.

25. Rebellious attitude and disposition towards ethics, authority, and the establishment.
26. Deficiency in the embracing of civilized and ethical values.
27. Bonded to iniquity and bitterness.
28. A pathology of soul.
29. Lost in mundane secularism.
30. Anti-Christian spirit.
31. Lost in idolatry.
32. Disregard for the Creator of the universe.
33. Self and others victimizing spirit.
34. Seeds of and proneness to violence (attitudinal and behavioral).
35. Enslaved to self-imposed ignorance.
36. Spirits of alienation and persecution.
37. Blind self-hatred.
38. Feeds on the sensate vanities and bitterness of secularism.

The above symptoms represent hatred, the influence of hatred or both. These influences of hatred are impacting on millions of lives in the American and World culture as well. This hatred manifested in these young adolescents and young adults must be given a top priority.

The volume of negativity, anti-social behavior and hatred among this young population, ought to be a wakeup call and an urgency to create a culture of social, economic, political, morale, ethical and spiritual health. This depravity of civility and pathology of soul warrants a top priority for the church, the community, and every level of government to get involved in creating health for this pathological cultural breeding ground.

Many of these hate filled young people are already victims and some will victimize others. There is individual and personal blame on the part of many of these young people. However, the society and the culture in which they like are not without blame. Since hatred is contagious, unpredictable, and dangerous it would be in the best interest of society to accept responsibility in developing resources and programs to produce healthy human beings, minimize and eliminate cultural environments that breed corruption, economic disparity, hatred and crime.

The public schools offer a great opportunity for teaching and instilling character education, ethical and moral values. The public schools are the place where most American children can be reached and taught. The U.S. Compulsory School Attendance Law requires children to attend school up to sixteen years of age. This is a golden opportunity to teach universal ethical and moral values along with other academic subjects.

Considering the massive disciplinary problems, youth crime and other destructive behavior on the part of American youth; character education, moral and ethical values must be required. In addition to requiring the courses in character education, ethical and moral values, special attention must be given to the character, ethical and moral values of the respective school board members, superintendents, administrators, as well as the classroom teachers. It is no secret, the educational administrators, teachers, and staff who interact with students and draw up the plans and educational policies and procedures, transmit their personal values and ideologies to the students and the educational system itself.

It is unwise, irresponsible, and criminal negligence in some cases to hire personnel who are morally, ethically, and ideologically unsafe to work with vulnerable youth. The custodial responsibility of vulnerable children, persons, minds, emotions, spirits, and bodies; must be appropriately and proactively vetted to avoid harm and irreparable damage.

It must be emphatically noted that the mental and spiritual health of students and teachers in the American public schools are grossly neglected. The utilization of addiction counselors, mental health counselors, social workers and chaplains are critically under represented and unavailable in most school districts. Drug use/ abuse, disciplinary problems and violence are on the increase in the public school system. Why this negligence? It is a form of insidious hatred.

The corrosion of moral and ethical values has made classroom teaching a health and safety hazard. Respect for teachers and the teaching profession has declined significantly. Teaching classes of twenty undisciplined children is very stressful. Unprofessional and unethical superintendents, principals, personnel administrators who so often subscribe to administration by intimidation place heavy stressful burdens on teachers.

Support for classroom teachers and the teaching profession, especially in urban areas, is declining. Therefore, at a time when teachers are in need of more support they are receiving less. Educational achievement is also hindered by confused and undisciplined students and demoralized teachers.

Educational achievement is also hindered by many other social changes. The traditional nuclear two parent family is impacted by single parent head of household families: parent working outside the home; deprived economic status of families, deterioration of neighborhoods and the decline of traditional church affiliation. The movement of more women into traditional jobs held by men and the seeking of gender equality with men is weakening the traditional influence and the rearing of children with more discipline and control.

There is a source of insidious hatred addiction influencing the interlocutory decline of the American people and their institutions. Reversal is possible.

Systemic Violations with Immunity

Camouflaged systemic hatred is so very damaging that it must be exposed to heighten the awareness of its existence. It is difficult to put a face on systemic hatred. People do not usually associate hatred with a recognized social agency or institution. It is much easier to identify a person who expresses hatred than an agency or an organization that expresses hatred. Individuals can be identified, complained against, arrested, jailed, taken to court and imprisoned. These legal remedies are not as applicable to an agency or an institution as they are to an individual. An agency or an institution cannot be arrested or incarcerated. However, these agencies and institutions can be vehicles of hatred and violations of human and Civil Rights.

When it comes to systemic hatred, the question must be asked; are agencies and institutions being used to shield, protect and defend haters? Are these agencies and institutions being used as a safe haven and sanctuary for individuals to commit hateful crimes with immunity?

Hatred is ill will. It may be covert (concealed) or overt (openly). Hatred is more transparent when individuals express it. However, ill will can be expressed through public policy, laws and administrative procedures. Hatred is expressed widely through administrative, judicial, and corporate institutions. These institutions often deprive citizens of the due process of law guaranteed by the U.S. Constitution.

It is routine for a principal or administrator to terminate the employment of a teacher without due process. Additionally, government administrators can put the terminated person on a no hire list and deprive such persons the opportunity of other future employment without any due process of law required by the U.S. Constitution.

The gravity of this hatred is realized when the terminated and violated individual attempts to get justice through the judicial system. In this case the terminated teacher and terminating principal are both U.S. citizens. The principal is given administrative immunity. The terminated teacher must sue the educational agency and not the principal who committed the termination and violations. The educational system provides defense for the principal against the terminated teacher.

This is an imbalance of justice in favor of the principal. This is a clear violation of the equal protection clause in the 14th Amendment of the U.S. Constitution against the terminated teacher. In the act of terminating the teacher, the principal has played, the roles of Violator (perpetrator), prosecutor, judge, and juror. The principal's dictatorial summary actions are supported and financed by the taxpayers. These arbitrary terminating actions of the principal are supported by the policy and procedures of the educational system and the state of jurisdiction. The net result of these actions is systemic hatred supported by the government against an innocent taxpaying citizen. The Terminated teacher has been robbed of job, benefits, equal employment opportunity, liberty rights, professional reputation, teaching career, economic security, and peace of mind.

How can these violations and victimization be done against a law-abiding citizen without any due process of law and be sanctioned by the U.S. Government and government agencies? How can the church and community be silent in the face of such gross dehumanization? These type violations are routine in many public schools and other government agencies.

Systemic hatred is real. It violated the U.S. Constitution, human rights and Civil Rights with impunity and immunity. Read Psychotrauma: The Human Injustice Crisis, for additional information.

Rejecting God's Gifts is Hatred

Hatred blinds individuals so severely that they don't see, appreciate, or understand the incomparable and unmatchable generosity of God. God provides a marvelous and mysterious creation that is witnessed by human life. God created man and woman and provided conditions to sustain life on a beautiful and bountiful earth. Individuals often allow hatred to shut out gratitude, even for their lives and existence. It is this kind of ingratitude that creates conditions and cultures of vicious and terroristic violence.

Jesus talked about how a certain man made a great supper and invited many (Luke 14:16-24). This certain generous man sent his servant to tell those who were invited to come. The invitees made excuses and failed to come to the supper. This kind man who had prepared the great supper became angry at those who used excuses not to come. This generous man extended his invitation to the poor, maimed, halt and blind. He found other persons to invite so that the supper would not be wasted. This generous man concluded that those who made excuses and failed to come would not taste of his supper.

God loved the world so much that he gave his only Begotten Son according to John 3:16. Jesus came unto his own, and (John1:11) says, "and his own received him not." There is a wide spread casual and lackadaisical rejection of the gifts and generosity of God. When a person who has been given the gift of life and existence and refuses the special gift of God in Jesus Christ, translates into being evil.

The rejector of God's gift may argue the point, that his life is his own; and he has the right to do with it whatever he wishes. No, God is the creator and owner of every individual life. When one refuses the special blessing of God, the refusal goes against the Will of God to the detriment of the rejecting person. It is hateful and evil to reject the special gift of God. Each individual is created to be a blessing to self and others.

When individual human beings reject the blessings of God, deficits, and sometimes curses, are created in their lives and the lives of others. The individual and corporate rejections of God's gifts for human life create hatred, evil, crime and corruption in the culture and the nation.

The consequences of the rejection of God and the gifts of God in the American culture is wreaking unprecedented hatred, crime, terroristic attacks, chaos, and confusion. Hatred does not happen in a vacuum. There are specific causes and reasons for hatred. There are specific reasons and causes for corrupt governments and corrupt societies. Mentally and spiritually disordered people create corrupt societies, sick and decaying cultures. These corrupt societies are characterized by secular idolatry, political corruption, social injustice, economic exploitation, inequitable developmental opportunities, and self-centered private religions.

It is no mystery behind the rise of terrorism and violence in America and the world. It is the results of rebellion against God and the disobedience to God's commandments and the rejection of God's gifts. Morally speaking, it is considered to be complimentary when we as people express pride in the evil that we do not do or have not done; we fail to consider the good that we did not do and could have, or should have done. We usually connect crime and corruption to what evil people do. Very seldom do we connect crime and corruption to our negligence, slothfulness, passivity, and indifference.

Civilized people, law abiding, and responsible citizens have the greatest potential to transform and enrich the American culture. Concerned American citizens must take the initiative to get rid of the breeding grounds for ignorance, hatred, crime and violence. The moral leaders with the moral conscience and moral compass must take the initiative and exterminate the breeding grounds for idolatrous ideologies, wickedness and evil. A wakeup call was given to America on 911 when hijacked American air planes crashed into the two towers of the world's trade centers in New York City and the Pentagon in Washington, D.C. killing over three thousand people. Since that time there have been continuous sporadic terroristic attacks on American soil.

It would be redundant and superfluous to identify all of the terroristic acts since September 11, 2001, tragedy that killed a total of 3066 people in New York, Washington, D.C. and in Pennsylvania. In addition to the human casualties on 911, there was over 6000 injured and over 10 billion dollars in infrastructure and property damage. To make the case on the lethal seriousness of hatred, four recent American terroristic acts will be portrayed for the years 2015,2016 and 2017. These following four acts of violent terroristic killings have overtones of race, religion, ethnicity, and gender. They provide graphic descriptions of hatred.

On June 17,2015, a 21-year-old white male entered the historic Emmanuel African American Episcopal Church in Charleston, S.C. and joined a group of about 12 Black men and women who were participating in a prayer meeting and Bible study class. Subsequently, this 21-year-old white man, Dylan Roof, systematically, shot and killed 9 persons in this group, including the pastor according to the Atlanta Journal Constitution and other news media.

On June 12, 2016, a 29-year-old man, Omar Mateen killed 49 people by shooting them to death in a gay night club in Orlando, Florida. Additionally, 58 people were wounded. This is a graphic illustration of hatred addiction. The sick need to maim and kill innocent people arises from within the hater. The victims provide a target where there is no excuse and no justification for such a crime. The addictive need is within the hater.

On October 1, 2017, Stephen Paddock, 64-year-old white male killed 58 people at a western music festival in Las Vegas, Nevada. Reports indicate that 500 people sustained injuries. The imagery Western music is not necessarily religious. However, it carries a certain persona associated with a certain group of people who appreciate Western music. Hatred addictive people are capable of creating in their heads their own symbolic dislikes and project them to whomever they wish. Irrational and insane hatred cannot always be rationally analyzed and diagnosed.

A Black American man, Emmanuel K. Samson, went to the Burnette Chapel Church of Christ in Antioch, Tennessee on September 24, 2017, shot and killed one person and injured 7 other persons.

The rising frequency of attacks on church parishioners seem to indicate a growing disrespect for religion, believers, and God. The church represents the people of God, the people of love, peace, nonviolence and justice. What kind of spirit would attack a loving and defenseless people in the house of worship? This growing hatred against religion, Christian believers and God is a very disturbing development in the American culture.

This disturbing development of hatred against the Church of Christ is forcefully demonstrated in Sutherland Springs, Texas on November 5, 2017 when 26-year-old Devin Patrick Kelley stormed the First Baptist Church with an assault weapon and killed 26 people. This was the worst mass killing in Texas' history. Again, this hatred targeted a benevolent, sacred place of peace and goodwill.

It is obvious and self-evident that hatred in general and hatred addiction is growing in America. It is significant to note that this hatred is being focused against the institution that represents love and goodwill, even towards the hater. Hatred against the church is not new in its long history. However, except for isolated instances of attacks against certain churches, as was the case of bombing of churches and burning of churches during the Civil Rights Movement in the 1950's and 1960's, America has not experienced this broad weapons assault against the people of the church in America.

Rejecting the gifts of God; Biblical knowledge and the love of Jesus Christ, conditions a culture for hatred. Beginning in the 1960's the U.S. Courts began to take prayer, Bible reading, character education and discipline out of the public schools. Depriving public school children of the knowledge of the Bible and public devotion to God creates a serious ethical, moral, and spiritual deficit in the American culture.

The deprivation of Biblical knowledge is much more serious than Americans are willing to acknowledge. In fact, too many Americans are in denial about God, about the revelatory knowledge of the Bible and the truth of Jesus Christ. The deprivation of this knowledge for children in the public schools in America is doing irreparable damage to the children and the Nation.

There is a correlation between the deprivation of God's word and the rise of hatred, human destruction and violence in the American culture. There is a reason behind the increase of terroristic violence, political corruption, education, and economic opportunity inequality. There is a reason why there is a rise in violence against religion and the church. There is a reason for the rise of hatred addiction in America.

The deprivation of Biblical knowledge corrodes democratic foundations, moral standards, ethical behavior, cultural enrichment, social responsibility, professional competence, human dignity, personal integrity, and the most noble purpose for living.

The above deprivations were not done in physical violent ways. They were done legislatively, judicially, administratively, bureaucratically, and with silent acquiescence and complicity. These vital cultural, spiritual, ethical, and moral values were taken away from public education without any physical violence and without any serious outrage or resistance.

Somehow, the Church and the American people, failed to see the hatred and continue to fail to see the hatred behind depriving children in the public schools Biblical knowledge, character education and moral discipline. How can the ministers, clergy and the church fail to respond to the serious admonition of the prophet Hosea: "My people are destroyed for lack of knowledge, I will also reject thee, that thou shall be no priest to me: seeing thou hast forgotten the law of thy God, I will also forget thy children (Hosea 4:6)." This knowledge referenced by Hosea means Biblical knowledge. Biblical knowledge is the basic foundation knowledge for living. Without the knowledge of God, all other knowledge is futile.

Governor Roy Barnes of Georgia signed House Bill 605 on April 23, 1999, that mandated Character Education to be taught from kindergarten through 12th grade in all public schools in Georgia. Many of the schools in Georgia failed to take this seriously. Atlanta Public Schools was one school district that did not implement this law in a serious manner.

There was no serious concern on the part of parents or the PTA (Parent Teacher Association), nor the church representatives. This indifference towards teaching character education, ethics and morals in many of the public-school districts in Georgia, including Atlanta Public Schools, is pervasive and perplexing.

There is another significant Georgia Law (20-2-148), entitled, Elective Course in History and Literature of the Old and New Testaments Eras (became law in 2007). Unfortunately, this is an elective course for 9th through 12th grade in Georgia, and it was left to the discretion of the respective district boards of education whether to include the course in the school curriculum.

Some school districts in Georgia have included this elective course in their curriculum. However, some school districts in Georgia have not included this elective course in their curriculum. Many appeals have been made to the Atlanta Board of Education to include the elective course in History and Literature of the Old and New Testament Eras in the Atlanta Public School Curriculum. Successive Atlanta Boards of Education have ignored the requests and refused to adopt the legal Bible Course in the Atlanta Public Schools Curriculum.

Again, this is an illustration of hatred addiction. The superintendents and school boards who ignore requests to include the greatest classical literature known to mankind in the school curriculum is serious hatred addiction against vulnerable children and humanity itself. Superintendents, boards and other officials and persons who deprive children, school systems and education of the Biblical validated knowledge upon which the Nation of America, the U.S. Constitution, Declaration of Independence, Pledge of Allegiance, democracy, The Motto-In God We Trust, were founded, is worse than treason.

The deprivation of Biblical education not only corrodes the foundations of America and the global culture and global moral compass; it separates minds, lives and souls from God. The deprivation of Biblical knowledge separates and alienates people from each other, themselves, and God. This depravation of the knowledge of God in the public schools and the deprivation of the acknowledgment of God in the public square is a relatively new and growing hatred in America. This deprivation of the knowledge of God in public schools and elimination of the public acknowledgement of God in the public square represent the worst cases of hatred in American history.

American slavery of African descendants beginning in 1619 at James Town, Virginia, represents one of the worst forms of hatred in history. However, the American institution of slavery did not seek to separate the slaves from the knowledge of God. The African American slaves had the freedom to worship and learn about God. It was the slaves' faith and belief in God that kept them spiritually and psychologically alive. Their faith and knowledge of God gave them hope to live and to overcome the bondage of slavery. It was the knowledge of God and the Bible that was most vital for their survival. The institution of slavery exploited and abused these downtrodden human beings. There is no evidence of laws instituted to deny the slaves, the emancipated former slaves from God or the knowledge of God. The key to their survival was their faith in God.

Laws restricting faith and discipline in the public schools started after the Brown vs Board of Education in May 1954, which outlawed segregation in the Public schools, predominately in the South. Before the decision of 1954 outlawing segregation in the public schools, the principals and teachers routinely had devotions in the classrooms, as well as in the school assemblies. The students participated in reading and reciting Bible Verses, prayer, and religious music. The principals, school faculty and students were free to talk about religion and discuss the Bible. This common practice in the public schools enabled many students to learn about the Bible and God. There were no laws, no public officials or community leaders prohibiting religious devotions and Bible discussions and recitations in public schools.

Biblical study and religious practice in the public schools of America have been declining progressively since the 1960s. It is having a serious detrimental impact. It is exacerbated by the influx of millions of diverse immigrants, cultural and religious pluralism. There is a significant decline in organized religion and church affiliation in America according to the PEW research. More significant and alarming; there is a growing resistance and intolerance to religion, and especially Christianity, in the public square. It is obvious, that secularism is growing and seeks to eliminate God, the Bible and the Christian practice out of the American culture.

In America in 2018, there is more integration, immigration, acculturation, toleration, accommodation, gentrification and modes of communication, transportation, and education of the population. And yet, there is more hatred in America than it was in the days of slavery, racial segregation, and discrimination. There is more hatred in America in 2018 than it was during the Civil War and the two world wars. Even during these wars, there was reverence for God in the American culture. When men were at their worst in those dark days, they still saw God at his best. There were no organized judicial efforts to shut God out. Many who were caught up in conflicts and wars repented and acknowledged their sins. The Negro slaves reverenced God by singing Negro Spirituals, "It's me, it's me, it's me O'Lord standing in the need of prayer. Not my brother, not my sister, but it's me O'Lord, standing in the need of prayer."

The two most illustrious Black American College Presidents, Booker T. Washington of Tuskegee University and Dr. Benjamin E. Mays of Morehouse College in Atlanta,

Georgia; gave Bible study, religion and Chapel services a prominent place in the educational curriculum and college life on campus. Booker T. Washington taught a Bible class to students in the college chapel each Sunday afternoon. He also taught a Sunday School Class at Greenwood Baptist Church at Tuskegee Institute Community. Dr. Benjamin E. Mays was President of Morehouse College for 27 years, from 1940 to 1967. Dr. Mays required daily chapel attendance of all Morehouse students during his tenure at Morehouse College. Dr. Mays also served as President of the Atlanta Board of Education upon his retirement from Morehouse. Dr. Mays was a mentor for Martin Luther King, Jr. and served as eulogist of Dr. King upon the death of Dr. King.

These two giant Black American Christian educators' philosophy of education merits serious attention and consideration. Biblical knowledge and faith in God had a central place in the lives and works of both of these renowned educators. Booker T. Washington emphasized the education of head, hands, heart and health. Dr. Benjamin E. Mays emphasized intellectual competence, moral solidity, and excellence in human relations.

These two educators provide the formulas, methodologies and challenges for love and successful living. The separation and alienation of theological education and faith in God from public education must be returned to save America, democracy, individual liberty, inalienable rights, and the people of God.

CHAPTER 5

Political Hatred

Let judgment run down as waters, and righteousness as a mighty stream. (Amos 5:24)

For we wrestle not against flesh and blood, but against principalities, against powers, against the rulers of the darkness of this world, against spiritual wickedness in high places. (Ephesians 6:12)

Woe unto them that call evil good, and good evil; that put darkness for light, And light for darkness; that put bitter for sweet, and sweet for bitter. (Isaiah 5:20)

But woe unto you, scribes and Pharisees, Hypocrites! For ye shut up the kingdom of heaven against men: for ye neither go into yourselves neither suffer ye them that are entering to go in. (Matthew 23:13)

Woe unto you also, ye lawyers! For you lade men with burdens grievous to be borne, and ye yourselves touch not the burdens with one of your fingers. (Luke 11:46)

Political Hatred

Reflections on the Political Process

Political hatred is the unethical and immoral misuse of the democratic system to promote selfish goals, unjust policies, and detrimental actions against the people at the taxpayers' expense. Political hatred is diabolical and dangerous because it is authorized to use the resources of the people fraudulently, mis representatively and unaccountably.

Political hatred has unlimited clandestine ways to devise evil schemes to exploit and express hatred through political systems of government and community. Political systems are authorized to make laws, interpret laws, and enforce laws. The election and appointment of public officials provide them with certain privileges, advantages, opportunities, and immunities. When these elected and appointed public officials become imbued with hatred and begin to misrepresent the people and promote themselves and their interest, political hatred corrupts the government and the society.

The privileges, notoriety and the rewards of political office become addictive. The sharing of unsavory favors become pleasurable and lucrative. These lucrative, partisan, fraudulent perks become an addictive cycle and way of life for the politician. Political favoritism becomes a partisan game without shame. As the political hatred addiction deepens, constituents are forgotten. The addiction progresses to the pathology of entitlement in the heads of the exploiting politicians.

The reason that political hatred addiction is so dangerous is because it has the potential to do more damage to the people and the system of government itself than other forms of addiction. Individual addiction is more limited, and self-contained. Political hatred addiction is corporate, systemic and operates at the head of the organization or respective political entity. A sick head makes the whole-body sick.

This progressive political addictive illness progresses to the point of transforming taxpaying citizens and voters into subjects to be misused, abused, and exploited. Citizens and voters are no longer respected as persons and citizens. They are subjects to be used and manipulated. Government for the people, by the people and of the people is no longer valid. It would be more accurate to say, government by the politicians, of the politicians and for the politicians. Political hatred addiction has brought America to this perilous point in this 21st century. Citizens have become the enablers.

The American citizens must realize that these perilous changes are not accidental. These perilous political changes are being designed and orchestrated with the use of taxpayer's money. Many of these government agencies hire expensive consultant groups to go on well-planned retreats to engage in governmental managerial, administrative, policy making techniques, philosophies, and strategies. They learn skills and techniques of deception.

In listening to an education board member's fascination after his experience at a consultant retreat workshop, was quite revealing. The board member expressed his delight when he finally learned at the retreat, "the difference between equity and equality." The education board member said with delight, "you can have equity without equality." I am sadly convinced that many of these government sponsored retreats compromise and take away significant human values. People can be programmed and scripted to practice hatred.

With the help of paid consultants, many politicians are learning to practice hatred with advanced skills.

Political hatred manifests itself in unethical campaign tactics, the corrosion of moral values and the violation of democratic principles. During political campaigns, it is not unusual to hear all manner of unsavory and even abusive accusatory language to discredit opponents in the political races. A lot of money is spent to paint negative and disparaging pictures of political contestants. Excessive demonization and vicious personal attacks are exchanged.

The expression of political hatred in American voter election process appears to be escalating. During and after the Donald Trump Campaign for the presidency, unprecedented hateful rhetoric filled the social media. In the 2017 Election a large number of women came forth and made allegation of sexual harassment.

The unprecedented number of women who came forth with sexual harassment allegations and within the 2017

Election context, suggest that this sexual harassment is used as political hatred.

The 2016 Presidential Election escalated political hatred interspersed with allegations of sexual harassment and other sexual misconduct against some of the candidates, including Presidential Candidate Donald Trump. After the election the expressions of sexual misconduct continued throughout 2017. The partisan use of sexual harassment permeated the news and took a great toll on a number of well-known men. Allegations of sexual misconduct is not new. Bill Cosby's case is still lingering somewhere in the judicial process. However, 2017 seems to have taken sexual harassment to a whole new level.

Judge Roy Moore, a candidate for a senatorial republican seat in Congress somehow precipitated an unprecedented number of women who came forth with allegations of sexual misconduct against Judge Moore dating back 40 years in Alabama. Also, John Conyers, a U.S. Congressman for five decades was the recipient of sexual harassment by women who came forth after decades. Other women are still coming forth against well-known men. Some of these celebrated men have been terminated from their positions. Other accused men are struggling to weather the storms of accusations.

The unprecedented number of women accusing Congressional men of sexual harassment prompted the House of Congress to pass an Anti-Harassment Training Measure on November 29, 2017 that requires lawmakers and aides to take annual anti-harassment training in response to the burgeoning allegations of sexual harassment against members of Congress.

No civil or fair-minded person would condone any sexual harassment or sexual misconduct toward women. However, when women come forth after decades of silence at a time when a person becomes a candidate for a national public office, such cases warrant some form of due process and objective fair hearings. Especially is this needed when there is such an atmosphere of partisan politics and hatred.

As an Equal Employment Opportunities Office of state government, there are some variables in allegations of sexual harassment that need investigating and assessing. There are a lot of discrepancies, discretions and arbitrary decisions involved in sexual harassment and sexual misconduct cases. Critical components of sexual harassment involves whether the perpetrated conduct was (1) invited, (2) solicited, (3) accepted, (4) approved, (5) mutual consented, (6) No clear rejection or complaint, (7) mutual friendship and favor. These are some elements to be examined in sexual harassment cases. Some men are blindsided by sexual harassment cases. Some men thought that their affection toward the woman was wanted, appreciated, and accepted. Most men and women are not infallible. Judicial care should be taken to safeguard the rights of men and women involved in sexual harassment cases. Many of these cases are expressions of political and partisan hatred.

It is sad commentary for the addiction of political hatred to begin with grown American Congressional Representatives.

Ethical, moral and character education training should begin at the pre-kindergarten stage. Such training should continue from kindergarten to elementary, middle school through high school. It is a tragedy to wait for old age to get this training as proposed for congressional members in November 2017. Character education and respect should be taught at the pre-kindergarten stage.

Divisiveness of Politics

In America and in the world, there are people against people. There are political parties against political parties. There are religions and ideologies against each other. There are races, social classes and nationalities against each other. There is a growing confusion in sexual roles and sexual identities in many societies and nations. This makes for a fertile political environment for political exploitation and group identity politics. This also creates conditions for the proliferation of hatred for political gain and personal benefits.

In the 2016 Election year of Donald Trump, unprecedented negative ads and social media were used in the pursuit of the U.S. Presidency. There was great resistance against the Trump Candidacy. The news media were replete on a daily basis with negative ads and stories against Donald Trump. Candidate Trump fought back with tweets labeling the mainstream news media as "Fake News." Upon the election of Donald Trump as the 45th President of the United States, the negative publicity, primarily from the mainstream media continued into his presidency for the whole year of 2017. The Robert Mueller Russian Collusion investigation continued through 2017. Additionally, there were women who came forth alleging sexual misconduct on the part of the President in past years.

The contagion of political hatred became evident when Roy Moore, a Republican Candidate from Alabama entered the race for U.S. Senate against the Democrat Doug Jones. Women came forth publicly alleging that Roy Moore had engaged in improper sexual conduct with them when they were teenagers. Roy Moore denied the allegations. The implication of political hatred is mentioned because some of the sexual misconduct allegations go back 30 and 40 years and surfaced a month or so before the election date of December 2017. These allegations against Roy Moore were used by some of the news media to revive the publicity regarding similar allegations against President Trump who supported the candidacy of Roy Moore. Although Roy Moore did not win the Senate seat, women are still coming forth with allegations of sexual harassment against well-known men after decades had passed.

It is the political motivation and the lack of due process that reveal the political hatred in the women coming forth with unsubstantiated sexual misconduct charges along with significant time delays. The negative information is irretrievably damaging whether true or false. The accused man is not the only one hurt and damaged by such Professional reputation and character damaging information.

In many instances, innocent family members and friends are damaged. Many instances, jobs are lost, opportunities are forfeited, and significant relationships are damaged. In some instances, health and lives are endangered.

Legislation is needed to protect law abiding citizens against arbitrary sexual misconduct allegations without the due process of law. The due process clauses in the U.S. Constitution must be strictly adhered to, and enforced if the integrity of Law is to be respected and maintained. This legal protection will help to limit the proliferation of political hatred. It is disappointing and infuriating that the human rights and Civil Rights of American citizens are so poorly and callously protected. The Fourteenth Amendment of the U.S. Constitution among other Amendments stipulates that no U.S. Citizen be deprived of life, liberty, or property without the due process of law.

It is no mystery that the epidemic of hatred is on the rise in America. The U.S. Constitution is not respected. It is violated daily. The courts are clogged up with unheard cases. The laws are often ignored, enforced, and adjudicated, arbitrarily, and unequally. These capricious judicial inequities create a breeding ground for hatred.

The political divisiveness along racial, religious, party, nationality and ethnic lines are growing in America. The divisions are fueled by political hatred. Although there is one America, Congress is seriously divided between democrats and republicans. Some democrats have been advocating for the impeachment of President Trump. Congressman John

Lewis of Georgia expressed reluctance in accepting President Trump as a legitimate president. Congressman Lewis also refused to attend the Opening Ceremony of the Civil Rights Museum in Mississippi in December 2017 because President Trump was scheduled to be at the ceremony. There are many other divisive examples and political animosity in the American government and among the American people.

The Transactional Analysis psychologists, Eric Berne and Thomas Harris put forth a credible theory that human beings have three ego states on which their behavior is based. It is called PAC (Parent, Adult, Child). The parent ego state develops rules and gives orders as parents do. The adult ego state exercises responsibility and takes care of business. The child's ego state does what children do. Children play and lack maturity and responsibility. Too many of our public officials are operating in the child ego state. Children are usually selfish and self-centered and do not see or understand the big picture beyond themselves. Apostle Paul acknowledged that when he was a child (I Corinthians 13:11) he spoke, understood, and thought as a child; but when he became a man, he put away childish things.

America faces from within and from without the most challenging and unprecedented problems of its existence. There is unprecedented hatred within and unprecedented hatred outside. These perilous problems and dangerous hatred require the utmost serious, competent, responsible, patriotic, God-referenced political leadership possible. The childish things must be put away. It is the child ego state, that is most vulnerable to hatred addiction. It is pleasurable to play the childish games of political hatred. The nature of addiction is to indulge in harmful behavior and enjoy the pleasure of such behavior with the awareness that the behavior is harmful. The pleasurable games played in the politics of hatred create division, weakens presidential leadership, and jeopardize the National interest and National security.

Many well-meaning Americans and others who profess to be Christians got caught up in the political hysteria of hatred against Donald Trump. This self-righteous political hatred became or has become so intense and irrational that many Americans who profess faith in God, have become critical and intolerant of Trump supporters and sympathizers. In their intolerant and judgmental minds, they feel that something is wrong with people who do not hate Donald Trump.

Biased News Media Casting Stones

The unprecedented derisive criticisms of Donald J. Trump, the 45th President of the United States cannot be reconciled with democracy, the Christian ethic, or the Gospel of Jesus Christ. This obsessive news media derision of President Trump is reminiscent of the mob behavior that created the climate that lynched thousands of African American men during the racially segregated era in America. This toxic derisive media frenzy against the Trump Presidency is also reminiscent of the hostile crowd that voiced their hatred to crucify Jesus Christ on the cross.

The hate-filled mob-like crowd cried out, "Crucify him," preferred the death of Jesus Christ, who was innocent rather than Barabbas, a convicted criminal. Hatred chose to crucify Christ and release Barabbas. This passionately expressed hatred towards President Trump by the biased news media is inordinately disproportionate to any compassion for the good of America. This expressed hatred is so all-consuming that it leaves no room for any compassion or consideration for helping the countless numbers of historically victimized Black African Americans or others who are in need. Media time and energy would be better spent on meeting the needs of the millions of needy and suffering people.

This one-dimensional media laser-focused hatred against President Donald Trump has lost sight of the serious multitudinous problems and unprecedented lethal threats to America and the world. The streets are filled with beggars, the homeless, drug addicts, mentally ill, criminal victimization, child abuse, child trafficking, failing schools, dysfunctional agencies, and innumerable social injustices. America and the world are plagued with unprecedented terrorism and nuclear ballistic missile threats. Considering all America's problems, it appears that some objective news media coverage is needed other than the superfluous hateful criticism of President Donald Trump. When the highest representative of the U.S. government is maligned, the whole U.S. government suffers.

Many people are deceived and negatively influenced by unprofessional, unethical and biased news media. This unprecedented ongoing criticism against President rump, not only damages him and impairs his ability to govern, but it imperils the Nation and the world. Lest the news media and others who are so inclined to deceive themselves completely with a variety of hypocritical contradictions and self-righteous proclamations, this Biblical pronouncement may be instructive, "He that is without sin among you, let him cast the first stone." (John 8:7) All people are flawed. Exacerbating Trump flaws damages the nation.

America has been blessed with some of the world's greatest educational, religious, political, and economic institutions. It has been among the nations that has produced the world's greatest inventions, champions, and leaders. It has participated in and won two world wars. It has provided more freedom to more people than any other nation perhaps in history. It has the longest lasting Constitution. The voices of truth, freedom and justice are urgently needed in America at this time in history to maintain the blessings of God. President Trump is also a child of God who needs prayer, respect, and constructive help. Damaging the President, damages the office of President and the Nation, itself.

Political Identity Abuse

Every American citizen and legitimate ethnic group is entitled to all the rights of citizenship and the equal protections of the U.S. Constitution. However, when individual citizens and groups claim and promote their special interests above other Americans and at the expense of the American people, this is abuse of democracy and a threat to the rights, freedom and equal opportunity and freedom of other Americans who are excluded.

This political identity abuse problem is already happening in America. It is producing and reinforcing political hatred addiction. These political identity factions are dividing the country. They are imparting partisan politics. There is a tug of war between the Democrats and the Republicans. The Republicans and their followers seek to take the country to the conservative right. The Democrats seek to take the country to the liberal left. There are political factions on both sides. From left to right and in between, there is growing hatred and confusion. Within the midst of this hatred, foundational values, democratic principles, ethical standards, sound doctrines and moral civility are being corroded. The corrosion of these survival values have destructive consequences for the Nation. It creates conditions for the growth of hatred addiction. Political hatred addiction has the potential to escalate out of control.

The democratic form of government in America allows for optimum individual freedom and autonomy. It allows for a free enterprise system. However, there are dynamic social, political, and cultural changes in America that threaten American freedom and democracy. Political and hatred addiction is at the core of this threat accompanied by Identity politics.

Identity politics allows for political factions to politicize and corrupt the democratic and Constitutional mandates of the

American government. The American Democracy is designed to be a representative form of government, by the people, of the people and for the people. It was not designed to promote personal and special interest groups.

The political hatred addiction is abusing democracy, the U.S. Constitution, the American Government, and the American people through corrupt identity politics. These political factions seek to gain political control through political corruption and selective favoritism. They are not willing to give America their highest patriotic allegiance under God. These political addictive haters elevate their ethnicities or special interests above America. However, they seek to use America and the tax payer's money and resources to elevate their special political identity and special interests.

Harmful Effects of Identity Abuse

The following enumerations are the results of political hatred addiction and special interest identity politics:

1. Many Americans are being selectively demonized for their political choices and personal beliefs. Some democrats express the view that something is terribly wrong with the Republican Party. Moreover, many Democrats express the sentiment that something is terribly wrong with Americans who vote for Republicans, and especially for Donald Trump. Many Republicans express the view that Democrats are

liberal to the point of jeopardizing America. These extreme political views of the major U.S. political parties create conditions for the increase of political hatred addiction.

2. Political hatred creates the abandonment of ethical, moral, righteous, just and democratic principles to win political races.

3. Political hatred contributes to the denial of truth, the neutralization of morality, the suspension of ethical standards, the dismantling of merit-based systems, immunity to accountability and the corruption of the judicial system.

4. Political hatred has incorporated economic greed to corrupt the democratic process in many governmental agencies. Public education is corrupted through government sponsored private and charter schools as one example.

5. Political hatred allows for the proliferation of unsound doctrines, undemocratic principles, unconstitutional actions, and alien ideologies that work against human values of freedom, truth, justice and civilization.

6. Political hatred squanders vital time, resources and energy on negative counter-productive capricious trivial pursuits and jeopardizes the security of the Nation from within and from without.

7. Political hatred weaponizes the government against democracy, Christian values, Biblical knowledge, and people who express their belief in God.

The seven enumerations above are not exhaustive. There are many other negative impactful things that could be said about political hatred addiction and political identity abuse. The reason that it can be concluded that they are negative and abusive is because they are incompatible with the principles of democracy, the truths of the Bible and the love of Christ. They represent unsound doctrines, injustice, and destructive practices. When political partisanism is promoted at the expense of American patriotism, that is a form of abuse, anti-American and anti-democracy.

Individuals are born with certain identities without their choice. Children do not choose their parents, their time of birth, their place of birth, their gender or sexual identity, their race, ethnicity, language, or country. In spite of all of these circumstances of birth, each child is a human being and a creation of God. After a child is born that child receives a name and other identities as he or she grows and develops in association with family and other human beings, agencies and institutions in the broader society and culture.

The child grows up and takes on many identities. In the American society, many young people choose a political identity of being a democrat, republican or independent. Some claim Christian, Jewish, Muslim or some other religious identity. Many youth follow the religious practices of their parents. God is not synonymous with religion. Religion is not synonymous with spirituality. There are many religions, ethnicities, and nationalities in America.

In America, many of the ethnicities, races, nationalities are politicized and abused. This happens when a particular ethnic religion, nationality or some other political group elevate their respective political interest above the interests of America and other citizens of America. This has become known as identity politics. Identity politics seeks special privileges, opportunities, and benefits at the expense of the general good of America and human welfare of all citizens.

Fallacies of Judging Others

Objective research will reveal the fallacies of judging others. Objective research will reveal that Republicans do not have a monopoly on racism, injustice, or hatred. Such objective research and study will also reveal that the Democrats do not have a monopoly on tolerance, ecumenism, inclusiveness, and universal brotherhood. Usually, extreme political judgments are one sided and biased.

Extreme political biased judgments must be addressed because they spread negative information and hatred. It feeds into the hatred addiction syndrome. This is hatred that takes on its own morbid autonomy. It is contagious and capable of escalating out of control and causing unpredictable damages.

Matthew 7:1-2, has a very insightful and enlightening perspective on judging others as follows: "Judge not that you be not judged. For with what judgment you judge, you shall be judged; and with what measure you mete, it shall be measured to you again."

What standard do you use when you make a judgment against another person? Do you hold yourself to the same standard? Usually, individuals who make judgments against others use their own self-righteous standards and find them bad. When such judgmental individuals use their own self-righteous standard to judge himself or herself, they find themselves good. That is the reason why Jesus said, "Judge not that you be not judged."

The person who makes a judgment exposes himself to be judged by his judgment. According to (Romans 10:2-3) those who use their self-righteous judgment are ignorant of God's righteousness. All persons are subjected to the standards and righteousness of God. All people fall short when subjected to the righteousness of God. All are sinners before God. God's righteousness cautions all persons about, "throwing stones," at others without examining self (John 8:7). Somehow, those who blame and stand in judgment of others can see the mote in the other person's eye and not the "beam" in their own eye (Matthew 7:3). Self-righteousness blinds us to our faults and personal defects.

Self-righteousness blamers often become self-righteous haters. Self-righteous haters can be extremely dangerous. The self-righteous hater imposes on himself selective blindness and selective deafness. This prejudicial and self-deceptive mental state, allows the self-righteous blamer and hater to see what he wants to see, hear what he wants to hear to confirm what he wants to believe. This self-deceptive and distorted mental disorder enable the blamer to perceive only the negatives about the hated person. The blamer and the hater has now "created" the picture and the desired perception of an individual who is wrong, bad, inferior, subhuman, demonic, undeserving, unworthy, and even evil.

This pathological self-righteousness and hatred concludes that such a person should be destroyed. The problem is that the "demonic person" is a fictional creation that was created in the disordered mind of the hater, and does not exist in reality. However, as W.I. Thomas, the American sociologist concludes in his, "Definition of the situation," that the perception may be false, in facts, but the consequences are real in reality.

It is important to see the transformation of the hater who is transformed into the real demon himself. There is a Scripture that says, "As a man thinks in his heart, so is he" (Proverbs 23:7). This would suggest that much attention must be given to the heart. This attention must be given to young hearts while they are impressionable and teachable.

It is also important to see and understand this pathology of self-righteousness. The self-righteous aspect allows the blaming and hating person to get a pathological pleasure and satisfaction from the hatred and the expressions of the hatred. This pleasure is derived from a feeling of self-righteousness - not self-wrongness. The hater does not admit or acknowledge the wrongness of his position. The established righteousness of God and the moral compass of God are so powerful and absolute, that they cannot be distorted or changed without the pathological distortion and insanity of the mind and the iniquity of the heart.

The hater, in an effort to distort and twist the reality of God's righteousness and justice, ends up distorting and twisting his own mind and corrupting his heart and soul. God's righteousness is real. There is a global and universal moral compass. It cannot be violated without consequences. There is a scale of justice. They are not arbitrary. The Bible teaches that righteousness and justice are established and ordained of God.

Personal opinions and self-righteous judgments without the righteousness of God and the moral compass of God, will lead to endless blame, hatred, confusion, conflict, chaos and catastrophe. It represents infantilism, insanity and a cesspool of hatred, corruption and wickedness. This happens to people and nations when they do not have clear Godly leadership. The book of Judges indicates a similar situation: "In those days there was no king in Israel: every man did that which was right in his own eyes" (Judges 21:25). A crisis in leadership in Israel over three thousand years ago does not approach the dangers the world faces in the 21st century when there is crisis in leadership. The component of technology makes the drastic difference. Among other armaments, the development of intercontinental ballistic missiles and nuclear weapons make the difference. The ability to transport and export hateful ideologies around the world makes the difference.

In the midst of all of this hatred and danger, the Bible reveals good news. There is a God of love who is the only Savior (Acts 4:12). He is the Prince of Peace, the mighty God, the Everlasting Father (Isaiah 9:16). He is King of Kings, and Lord of Lords (Revelation 19:16). He is the way, the truth (John14:6) and the life. God has given every man, woman, and child more than a righteous and just leader; more than a moral compass. God has given the abundant and eternal life (John 3:16) to everyone who will receive the gift.

When judging and evaluating our public officials and leaders; we must be humble and sufficiently objective, to search our own hearts, minds, motives, and personal contributions. Do I as a critic, have anything better to offer than criticism and condemnation? How do I fit into the equation, the person, and circumstances I am criticizing and condemning? What is hindering my contribution? Have I been infected with the contagion of political hatred addiction?

It is difficult to find a rational positive benefit of hatred towards others and self except for the selfish pathological need to harbor it and express it. Elevation, edification, reparation, and restoration are better options than condemnation. The critic must evaluate his or her own contributions and responsibility before criticizing and condemning others.

Public Theological Perspectives
God has Set the Standards

The government, all public officials, and leaders of the people, in order to be legitimate, must accept the authority and the sound doctrines of God as revealed in the Bible. The Bible is God's historically validated special revelation to all mankind. God has set the standards and the laws to govern the conduct and behavior of mankind. It is absurd, preposterous, and sacrilegious for any man to ignore God's laws and God's authority. Manmade laws that are contrary to God's laws and God's authority lead to destruction and death. God's laws are inescapable. They are established in creation and in "God's Only Begotten Son, Jesus Christ. God has declared his approval and his pleasure in his creation and in his Only Begotten Son. God is the Creator and source for religion, law, art and science. Psalm 24:1 declares that "The earth is the Lord's and the fullness thereof, the world and they that dwell therein." 1 Corinthians 3:11 says, "For other foundation can no man lay than that is laid, which is Jesus Christ." Stop the absurdity!!!

Religious Liberty and Free Speech

When money and the material things of this world become your idol god, you not only lose your religious liberty and freedom of speech, but your soul is also lost in the process. When a person is willing to give up his religious liberty, freedom of speech and his soul for material gain; that person has not only given in to evil, but has also joined the forces of evil. When public officials join the forces of evil, they jeopardize society, humanity, and all of us. Unfortunately, there is no neutral or safe place for any of us. We are either working for evil or working against evil. Ethical neutrality, moral indifference and passive aloofness are great dangers to life, liberty, and the blessing of God. First Timothy 6:10-12 gives helpful insight and instruction: "For the love of money is the root of all evil, which while some coveted after, they have erred from the faith, and pierced themselves through with many sorrows. But thou, o man of God, fee these things; and follow after righteousness, godliness, faith, love, patience, meekness. Fight the good fight of faith..."

Greatest Book and Supreme Law

The Word of God in the Bible supersedes the U.S. Constitution and all other manmade laws. The Bible is the Book from God to mankind that has authority and jurisdiction over all mankind in all places and to all generations in heaven and in earth. The hierarchy of Biblical administration is through Jesus Christ, the Holy Spirit and the Church of Christ. The Church receives its orders from God, the Father, Son and Holy Ghost. Every soul is subject unto God. God's message is for every person and every nation. The people of God and the Church bow only unto God. God requires all persons and all nations to bow to God. This includes all kings, emperors, queens, presidents, supreme courts, leaders, constitutions, and manmade laws. The Bible is superior to the U.S. Constitution and all other manmade laws. All human beings, men and women are first and foremost creatures of God, not of the state, the nation, secular society, or any creature. God is the sole owner of human beings. Therefore, all men and all nations are accountable to God and subject to the Supreme Laws of God, And the consequences for violations.

America Needs a Godly Leader

America needs a presidential leader who is guided by truth, justice and peace, not by power, wealth and greed. America needs a leader who believes in the just laws of the U.S Constitution for every U.S. citizen; and not for the political favoritism or special interest elitism. America needs a leader who believes that each person should be judged by their content of character and individual merit as a person, and not by their race, ethnicity, or any other circumstance of life. America needs a just, moral, ethical, and righteous leader who will commit the Nation to the long overdue restoration for the racially disadvantaged loyal Black Americans. America needs an honest leader who demonstrates patriotic love for America and respect for all humanity. America needs a courageous leader who will stand up for the biblical word of truth and the God given unalienable rights of religious liberty and freedom of every person; and represent America as a Nation under God. America needs a leader who will exercise

Godly responsible stewardship over the lives, resources, gifts, opportunities, and blessings of God on the earth. God has blessed America in giving its citizens a right to vote to select its president and other public servants. Use your vote wisely, sacredly, and prayerfully.

The Righteousness of God is Standard

God has already set the standards for his righteousness for all mankind. It is perilous and dangerous to substitute the righteousness of man for the righteousness of God. Therefore, it is a primary responsibility for every person to learn the righteousness of God standards as set by God. This is vitally important because Proverbs 14:12 says, "There is a way which seemeth right unto a man, but the end thereof are the ways of death." Romans 10:2-3 confirms what Proverbs says in the following words, "For I bear them record that they have a zeal of God, but not according to knowledge. For they are being ignorant of God's righteousness, and going about to establish their own righteousness, have not submitted themselves unto the righteousness of God." Religious and political zeal without the righteousness of God and without the knowledge of God's Word, is perilous and deceptive. When people deviate from the ways of God, like sheep without a shepherd, they go astray. Judges 21:25 gives insight into self-righteousness in the following verse, "In those days there was no king in Israel: every man did that which was right in his own eyes." Thanks be to God for giving humanity a righteous king in Jesus Christ. Follow King Jesus, the Christ. He is the moral global compass.

It must be noted that God gives human beings the autonomy of free will to make personal decisions. God does not force anyone to believe in God or to believe in Jesus Christ. here is no such thing as forcing anyone to become a God believer or Christ believer. No person is born a Christian. It is each individual's personal choice to believe or not believe; or to accept or reject.

American Democracy and Public Theology

The 1st Amendment of the U.S. Constitution prohibits a theocratic form of government in the name of religion. America has a democratic form of government that was created by a philosophy of Judeo-Christian doctrines. The American Democracy proposes to be a representative form of government for the people, by the people and of the people. It is the longest lasting constitution of any other known government.

It is significant to note that Christian believers developed the American democratic form of government and constitution on September 17, 1787, at a time when there was no significant heterogeneity in America besides the native Americans and the Negro slaves. It is significant that these Christian believers developed a universal constitutional form of government that was inclusive of all people. However, the practice of this democracy excluded Black African

American Slaves at this time in history. Religions do not have a monopoly on the universal moral and ethical principles essential for the equitable administration, allocation, distribution and accountability for the goods, resources and services existing in the society. Therefore, the laws of the U.S. Constitution were not "religious" laws, but they were laws in congruence with truth, justice, and righteousness.

God created and God requires specific laws and commandments to govern the conduct of all people regardless of their form of government or type of religion. God requires all leaders and all people to live according to the truth, justice, righteousness, goodness, mercy, love and the will of God. God's laws and principles are not arbitrary and do not depend on individual opinion for their validity. God's laws and principles are true, just, righteous and based in reality. God's laws are not relative, neutral or fictional. They are real with real consequences. No person, nation or religion is exempt from God's laws and judgment.

God is the creator of the universe with absolute jurisdiction over everything and every being (Genesis). The earth and everything therein belongs to God (Psalm 24). God demands that every soul be subject to God (Romans 13:1). Contrary to the expressions of many judges and legal scholars, religion is not synonymous with God, the Bible or Jesus. Religions are created and born in history. They also die in history. However, God, the Bible and Jesus Christ are above history and human culture. The autonomous nature of man made by God, has free will to choose. Man can choose to ignore God, Jesus, and the Bible. However, man's independent negative choice does not negate God, Jesus, or the Bible. Man's independent choice does not excuse man's duty to obey God and God's commandments. Man's autonomous free will does not excuse man's rebellious spirit against God. God's jurisdiction is inescapable. His commandments cannot be suspended. Personal responsibility and accountability to God cannot be delegated or evaded. God's divine laws and natural laws are absolutely supreme. MANMADE LAWS ARE ONLY VALID WHEN THEY ARE CONGRUENT WITH GOD'S LAWS & WILL.

CHAPTER 6

Tragedy of Racial Hatred

And hath made of one blood all nations of men for to dwell on all the face of the earth, and hath determined the times before appointed, and the bounds of their habitation. (Acts 17:26)

There is neither Jew nor Greek, There is neither bond nor free, there is neither male nor female; for ye are all one in Christ. (Galatians 3:28)

He hath showed thee O man, what is good; and what doth the Lord require of thee but to do justly, and to love mercy, and to walk humbly with thy God. (Micah 6:8)

Render therefore to all their dues: tribute to whom tribute is due; custom to whom custom; fear to whom fear; honor to whom honor. (Romans 13:7)

If my people, which are called by my name, shall bumble themselves, and pray, and seek my face, and turn from their wicked ways; then will I hear from heaven, and will heal their land. (2 Chronicles 7:14)

Tragedy of Racial Hatred

Circumstances of Birth

The circumstance of birth is a great determiner of who you are and what you believe. Circumstances of birth determines your parents, socio-economic status, your race, your name, your nationality, your values, your belief system, your physical characteristics, your potentials for growth and development. The culture that a person is born and reared in provides their identification, perceptions of self, others, and the world.

There are numerous things that make up the identification and characteristics of individuals of which they had no control. Therefore, it is insensitive and cruel to hate and hurt someone based on personal identification and characteristics of which they had no control.

Hierarchy of Human Needs

Maslow's Hierarchy of Needs illustrate the impact of prolonged discrimination and oppression against an identified group of people. (Figure 1.1) The vast majority of people are at the bottom of the triangle because they are preoccupied with meeting the primary and basic needs for physiological needs and safety needs. Most do not have the time nor the resources to climb the socio-economic ladder to meet advanced social needs, self-esteem, and self-actualization needs. The people at the bottom spend their time, energy and meager resources to survive the overt and covert hatred that keeps them down, underdeveloped, and unfulfilled. The great God given potentials of the majority of Black Americans have been oppressed, dissipated and wasted away. This is an ongoing human tragedy for all Americans and all people.

Maslow's Hierarchy of Needs

1. Where are you located on this hierarchy of needs?
   _____.

2. Where would you prefer to be on this hierarchy of needs?

   _____.

Figure 1.1

Triangle of Victimization

The Karpman Triangle (Figure 2.1) further illustrates the tragedy of racial hatred in America. The Karpman Triangle illustrates three roles on the three sides of the triangle. It has the persecutor role who makes victims and the rescuer role who helps the victim. The Karpman drama triangle illustrates the vicious cycle of persecution, victimization, and rescue.

Although, the victims may be innocent and the rescuers heroic, the triangular vicious cycle is pathological. Who are the persecutors? Who are those persons who make victims? Who are the persecutors and how did they come to be persecutors? Who are these rescuers? What would rescuers be doing if they were not rescuing victims? Why is this drama pathological triangle perpetuated?

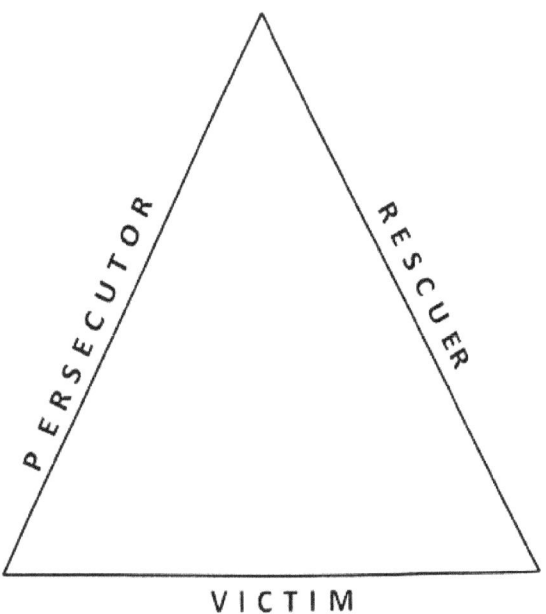

The Karpman Triangle

1. What role do you play in this triangle?

    _____ .

2. Which role do you prefer to play? Explain

    _____ .

3. Have you played all of these roles? Explain

    _____ .

Figure 2.1

Black Americans' U.S. Contributions

After the American Civil War and the issuance of the Emancipation Proclamation, that was an opportune time to provide compensatory support and reconcile the alienated races. That did not happen. After the Emancipation Proclamation, the freed Negroes were at the bottom of the socio-economic ladder and in poverty-stricken destitution. However, racial segregation and discrimination were improvements over outright slavery. The freed Black Americans capitalized on this newly granted freedom and built communities, churches and schools.

During this time after 1865, Black Americans were ready to join white Americans in the great reconstruction after the civil war, because the predominant Black population harbored no hatred towards whites. They believed in the Bible, Jesus Christ and God and embraced an ethic of forgiveness. However, there was no time to forgive and build new humans and constructive relationships, because the hatred by White Americans continued and in some cases accelerated. Although, Black Americans had been emancipated, there was no such thing as social, economic, political or racial equality, especially in the South.

The tragedy of this racial hatred, inequality and oppression; not only hurt the Black Americans, but all America as well. These legally freed offsprings of slaves were among the most gentle, industrious, patriotic Americans, and civilized

Christians in the world. The Black Americans helped to build the most powerful and the most blessed country on earth.

Black Americans during and after slavery, worked in the homes and on the plantations of white Americans. They cooked, cleaned, provided childcare, nursing care, maintenance and all manner of domestic labor and plantation services. Black Americans have fought and died in all the American wars and international conflicts.

During the hundred-year period, from 1865 to 1965, no other people on earth has done more than the American Negro with so little and against such great odds. To mention a few accomplishments, they built communities, churches, schools, colleges, and universities. They produced outstanding scholars, and world renown heroes such as Booker T. Washington, George Washington Carver, Benjamin E. Mays, Thurgood Marshall, Martin Luther King, Jr., Joe Louis, Mahalia Jackson, and a host of others. These renown Black Americans were produced during the segregation period in America.

America and the world have been blessed by the contributions of the Black Americans. Extraordinary credit must be given to Black Americans for their accomplishments in a demeaning and racially discriminatory society. The underutilization of the Black American potential due to individual and systemic related hatred and injustices is an ongoing American tragedy.

America, in this twenty first century, has already lost irretrievably, a God gifted treasure of an indigenous loyal, faithful, and patriotic people in the Black Americans. This treasure has been lost due to the continuing one hundred fifty years of disappointment to the Black Americans in achieving or being granted social justice and equality in America. Drastic social, political, moral, educational, and ethical values have changed in America the past 50 years (beginning about 1970). Hispanics have outnumbered Black Americans during this period of time, LGBT, and other religions outside of Christianity have become politically influential. The technology of social media influences the thinking and values of the American society. Other minorities have usurped and diluted much of the priority and entitlements of Black Americans.

The sacrifices made primarily by Black Americans to get the enactment of the 1964 Civil Rights Act turned out to be disappointing. It was disappointing because other groups who were never enslaved and deprived as Black Americans benefited from the 1964 Civil Rights Act. This law was extended to women, national origin, Age groups, religion, color, and sexual gender. This diluted the effectiveness in helping Black Americans to overcome discrimination in employment and other areas.

In addition to eliminating merit-based systems and affirmative action in employment, they are subjected to arbitrary and biased decisions of employment agents and agencies. The arbitrary and biased decisions are more detrimental now, post the 1964 Civil Rights Act, for Black Americans due to integration and immigration. In the segregated society, Blacks had a monopoly on jobs that served Blacks. White Americans had no interest in working in Black schools and other Black agencies and institutions. Before 1964 there was not significant numbers of other races in the south who competed for jobs in the Black community. Also, during this pre-Civil Rights era, there was often a generous good grace paternalism that worked in favor of the Black Americans.

Social Change and Moral Decline

The advent of Civil Rights, massive immigration, increased advanced technology, LGBT and ecumenical movements have brought about significant social change and a shift in traditional moral values in America in 2018. These changes in moral values have exacerbated the problems for Black Americans due to the unstable and fluctuating moral compass. All Americans are adversely impacted by these changes in moral values.

During and since the days of American institution of slavery, Black Americans invested their hope in justice, righteousness, and truth. These are not Black American values. They are universal values for all human beings. The current trending social changes in America, are embracing moral relativity, ethical neutrality, political corruption, administrative intimidation, intellectual incompetence, and spiritual arrogance.

Dr. Martin Luther King, Jr. gave America and the world a great moral and spiritual boost. Dr. King was able to provide extraordinary moral, ethical, and spiritual leadership for America and the world because of the moral, ethical, and spiritual richness of the Black African American culture that produced him. The rich moral, ethical, and spiritual values promulgated by Dr. King are not new or unusual in the Black African American heritage.

The core tragedy of racial hatred towards Black people in America ignored and rejected the most profound survival values known to mankind. Dr. Martin Luther King, Jr. is just one expression of thousands upon thousands of Black Americans who want and desire to share these God given values of peace, justice, freedom and love with America and the world. Blind racial hatred rejects those people and those values that are trying to reach and save them and America.

In 1895, on September 18**, Booker T. Washington, President of Tuskegee Institute, in Alabama, gave his electrifying speech to a predominant white audience, "Cast Down Your Buckets Where You Are." Over 120 years ago Booker T. Washington reached out to the white Southerners and America on behalf of Black Americans.

His plea and appeal to this white audience can be summarized in part by paraphrasing, "We black people have proved our loyalty to America and the South. We have built your cities and railroads. We have harvested your crops and cared for your children and elders. We want to work in partnership with you for the common cause of America. We know each other. Let us help you prosper our people and the nation." The speech that Booker T. Washington gave in 1895 is in his book, Up From Slavery.

The ultimate tragedy of racial hatred is that it has hindered the development and utilization of the God given talents and potentials of Black Americans and deprived America and the world of these redemptive gifts of God. Racial hatred is also changing the moral, ethical, and spiritual values of Black Americans.

The rich soulful cultural and spiritual values that produced men and women like Booker T. Washington, George Washington Carver, Paul Robeson, Joe Louis, Benjamin E. Mays, Martin Luther King, Jr., Harriett Tubman, Mahalia Jackson, Rosie Parks and others are being diluted and diminished. Many Blacks are beginning to harbor racial hatred themselves.

The good news is that these glorious values of God from our past can be resurrected and revive our spirits, our souls and our future in God. The reality of the resurrection of Jesus Christ remain our undying hope and the hope of the world.

A Medley of Black American Soul Music

The Black African Americans enrich the culture, spirit and soul of America and the world with their music of spiritual hope. This unique music embodies the stories and the rich spirits and souls of a people who kept faith and hope in God. It is a window into their tragic bondage and souls. It reveals their American story and their moral and spiritual foundations for survival. It is significant that a people who were hated so vehemently, did not incorporate hatred in their music. They expressed their suffering without hatred, vengefulness, or condemnation.

The Black American Spirituals have a wealth of knowledge, cultural enrichment, ethical lessons, moral standards and human inspiration.

The following is a medley of titles of Negro Spirituals or Black African American Spirituals originated from the Black African American enslavement and oppression in America:

1. Sometimes I feel Like a Motherless Child.
2. Soona Will be Done with The Troubles of the World.
3. I've Been In the Storm so Long.
4. Way Down Yonder By Myself, I couldn't Hear Nobody Pray.
5. Nobody Knows the Trouble I've Seen.
6. Some Glad Morning When this Life is over, I'll Fly Away.
7. Every Time I Feel the Spirit Moving in My Heart, I will Pray.
8. I Heard of a City Called Heaven. I am Trying to make that city my Home.
9. O'What A Beautiful City.
10. Swing Low, Sweet Chariot, and Let Me Ride, I've Got A Mother on the Other Side.
11. Steal Away to Jesus. Steal Away Home.

12. We are Climbing Jacob's Ladder.
13. Keep your Hands on the Plow, and Hold on.
14. There is a Balm in Gilead that is Good for Sin Sick Souls.

The messages of these entitled songs can be very educational for all people interested in the plight of humanity. However, these songs are more than educational lyrics. There is a transmittable spiritual, moral, and inspirational content, that is relevant for intellectual growth and spiritual enrichment. They contain spiritual gifts and special blessings from God to heal and restore Americans to wholeness. The music and the message of the Negro Spirituals are inspired by God. They are good for the healing of confused minds, hate filled hearts and sick souls. They are good for the healing of the Nation.

There are no other people outside of Israel whose history of human bondage and oppression reflect more the hand and the love of God. When the Black enslaved African Americans were at their worst levels of degradation and suffering, they saw God at his best, even though these severe trials and tribulations. They loved God with such purity, trust and depth, that they did not hate their white American slave masters. As Jesus on the Cross, these rare souls of God uttered from their God touched spirits, "Father, forgive them, for they know not what they do." Black Americans are the most loyal Americans.

Capturing the Spirit of Negro History

As we recapture and incorporate the God inspired Negro History in America, we enlighten and empower ourselves and America, we enlighten and empower ourselves and world. Negro History in America has great lessons for productive living and survival values. All Americans and other people of the world would receive great benefits by studying Black American History. The study of the Negro Spirituals, The Negro Church, the Negro writings, and inventions have Great enriching benefits for humanity. The study of the Black American Heroes, such as Booker T. Washington and Martin Luther King, Jr. has the potential to make a significant Positive difference in our culture and the world. It is quite evident that Negro (Black) American History is universally significant because God worked in this history to save People that the world abandoned and forgot about. The Negro American story is about a People who survived by their soul power and faith in God.

Urgent Need for Black Deprived Youth Accelerated Compensatory Education

Human beings have a human right to knowledge and education to sustain life and a livelihood to keep them from perishing. A large number of Black youth are being deprived of a quality education. Many of them are depriving themselves. Many of these youth are being inadequately educated. The deprivation of education and the means of making a livelihood is genocide. A quality education, along with the technological tools for work and a just opportunity for employment are essential for a sustainable livelihood and life, itself. The high rate of school suspensions, dropouts, educational failures, lack of economic opportunities, lack of moral and spiritual guidance, are destroying our youth and our future. Educational institutions must immediately make accelerated compensatory quality education a top priority for God's children and citizens of America. Compensatory involves the necessary supports, additional personnel, and services to concentrate and speedup the educational process for the students who are deprived and behind. The deprivation of a quality education is equivalent to the deprivation of life, itself. This urgent educational need must be considered an emergency requiring immediate attention.

The Way Out of Darkness
(The Spiritual Domain, page 120)

It is most unfortunate that somewhere along the way, the American public educational system divorced itself from the formal teaching of the Bible and Christianity in the schools. The subsequent spiritual/Christian knowledge deficit has significantly imperiled the spiritual and ethical health of the nation and the world. It is unwise, irresponsible, and dangerous to educate minds and ignore the ethical, moral and spiritual guidance of those minds. Human beings possess moral and spiritual guidance of those minds. Human beings possess moral and spiritual capacities. Our educational systems have allowed these spiritual and moral capacities to exist as vacuums. Since "Nature abhors a vacuum," these neglected and empty capacities are being filled with alien moralities and evil spirits.

It is the challenge of public theologians to seize upon this opportunity to this late time in history to specialize and major in the spiritual domain in transmitting the highest ethical, moral, and spiritual knowledge known to mankind. It is the incomparable revelatory good news knowledge of the Holy Bible, which culminated in the salvation knowledge of Jesus Christ. This is the knowledge that must fill the vacuums of the heart soul and spirits of this misguided, confused, and lost generation.

The World's Most Valuable Knowledge

The most valuable knowledge in the history of mankind is the knowledge about God. The Bible is God's Special Knowledge of Revelation to Mankind. Underneath, the Bible is man's search for God. From above, it is God's revelation and self-disclosure to mankind. The Bible is knowledge about the ultimate purpose of human existence. The Bible is the Book of Truth, knowledge, Wisdom, Righteousness, Justice, Mercy, Hope, Faith, Goodness, Forgiveness, Freedom, Healing, Grace, Law, Peace, Love, Restoration, Redemption, Salvation,

Light and Life. The Bible is the Book of God's Ways, Will and WORD Made Flesh in the Savior, JESUS CHRIST. The Bible is Divine, Transcendent and Spiritual Knowledge. This spiritual Knowledge from God can be used through Faith to enable and empower the believer to overcome the tragic predicament of sin, suffering and death. The Bible is the true story of God's visitation into the history of mankind to deliver God's Message of Love and God's Son of Salvation. God's Message is to every soul, including YOU.

CHAPTER 7

Hatred Addiction

Beloved, believe not every spirit, but try the spirits, whether they are of God. (1 John 4:1)

Wherefore gird up the loins of your mind, be sober. (1 Peter 1:13)

Be sober, be, vigilant; because your adversary the devil, as a roaring lion, walketh about, seeking whom he may devour. (1 Peter 5:8)

For the good that I would I do not; but the evil which I would not, that I do. Now if I do that I would not, it is no more I that do it, but sin that dwelleth in me.
(Romans 7:19-20)

Hatred Addiction

Symptoms of Chemical Addiction

The following symptoms of drug abuse, dependence and addiction are based on the guidelines of NIDA (National Institute on Drug Abuse), DSM-V (Diagnostic Statistical Manual of Mental Disorders), NAADAC (National Association of Alcohol and Drug Addiction Counselors), ASAM (American Society of Addiction Medicine, GACA (Georgia Addiction Counselors' Association) and professional Clinical practice.

There are eight basic symptoms of drug addiction. They are enumerated without extensive elaboration just to acquaint the readers of this work as to what they are.

1. Compulsive use of substance.
2. Obsessive preoccupation related to use.
3. Tolerance change to increased quantity and frequency.
4. Denial system (psychological) of dependence.
5. Blackouts (Memory lapses).
6. Withdrawal syndrome (Discomfort without drug).
7. Progressive condition (Requires detoxification).
8. Chronic condition (Requires Abstinence and treatment).

Chemical abuse, dependence and addiction are listed in the DSM-4 and DSM-5 as mental disorders. The Diagnostic Statistical Manual of Mental Disorders is published by the APA (American Psychiatric Association). The authors and contributors to the DSM consist of over two hundred medical doctors, psychiatrists, and psychologists.

These validated symptoms of chemical abuse, dependence and addiction are presented to gain insight into hatred addiction. There are similarities between drug addiction and hatred addiction.

Predictable Consequences of Addiction

There are five predictable consequences of drug addiction. These five predictable consequences are known as, "The five D's of Doom." Dementia is the first D of doom. Dementia denotes brain damage and mind impairment. This cognitive impairment results in impaired judgment and intellectual incompetence.

The second D of doom is detention. The impaired mind and impaired judgment frequently results in violations of the law or conflicts that lead to unlawful behavior and referral to the criminal justice system or some inpatient facility for the mentally ill.

The third D of doom is dysfunctionality. The addicted person regresses to irresponsibility and lack of skills and competence to perform satisfactorily in employment or self-care and management.

The fourth D of doom is dependence. Dependence on others for livelihood, support and maintenance is often the place where the addicted person ends up. And of course, the final D is death. Death is hastened by many factors related to addiction.

It is obvious that the outcome of addiction is progressive deterioration in all areas of life. Addiction is primarily a brain disease triggered by the use, abuse, and indulgence of mind altering and brain damaging chemicals.

There are significant correlations between chemical addiction and hatred addiction. They both involve the neurotransmitters (messengers) of the brain. The cognitive and emotional impact of hatred on the brain impacts feelings, thoughts, and behavior.

Guidelines for Drug Detoxification

Detoxification means to get the toxic drugs out of the system safely. There are two types of detoxification - ambulatory and inpatient. Ambulatory is the walk in and out type of detoxification that does not require remaining as an inpatient to get the detox medications. Inpatient detoxification is required when there is a detrimental risk of life-threatening withdrawal syndrome. The withdrawal syndrome is the disruptive and detrimental reaction of the body when the addictive drug goes out of the body. It is not commonly known, but withdrawal from certain drugs can be life threatening.

Depressants, sedatives, and tranquilizing type drugs, such as alcohol and valium, in many cases require inpatient detoxification. Withdrawal from depressant drugs can be severe and life threatening. Symptoms of withdrawal from depressants include shakes (tremors), hallucinations, seizures, D.T.s (delirium tremens), accompanied with elevated vital signs. Remember, addiction to depressant drugs can be life threatening when they go out of the system unreplenished. To avoid the painful and life-threatening withdrawal is why many persons continue to use and abuse drugs to avoid the withdrawal syndrome.

There are six categories of abused drugs. They are (1) Depressants, (2) Stimulants, (3) Narcotics, (4) Hallucinogens, (5) PCP (Phencyclidine), and (6) Inhalants/ Aerosols. The depressant drugs have the highest priority for detox in cases of dependence and addiction. This includes the depressant drug, alcohol, which is a legal drug.

Current Opioid Crisis and Alcohol

Although alcohol kills more people, opioids are considered to be the major drug crisis in America, beginning in 2015. The reason alcohol is not considered a crisis in America is because it is rare that a person overdoses on alcohol. The reason that alcohol overdosing is rare, it is because the depressant drug causes the consuming person to go to sleep before the lethal toxic level of blood alcohol concentration is reached. Whereas the consumer of the opioid narcotics do not have that safeguard of passing out before the lethal toxic level is reached.

Drug Abuse Effects

All mood-altering drugs, including marijuana, have effects on the neurotransmitters of the brain. When the "messengers" of the brain are affected, the mind, emotions and behavior are impacted. The fine-tuned healthy brain can be put at risk for dementia, distorted sensibilities and altered perceptions of the world of sobriety, sanity, civility, and the world of reality.

It is clear that the cost of recreational drug use and abuse not only outweigh the benefits, but this immature indulgence is also unaffordable and jeopardizes the nation.

The Nature of Hatred Withdrawal

The poison or toxins of hatred are not chemicals or material things. However, it cannot be denied that hatred is toxic, and hatred is real. Hatred may be invisible, but its toxic and wickedness have daily vivid and explosive violent impact in the world of audible and visible reality every day. Hatred addiction is characterized by being self centered, irrational, insidious, controlling, intolerant and violent. Hatred addiction is known to impair judgment and violate legal, ethical, moral and civilized values. It inhabits the mind, heart and emotions and takes control of the hatred addicted person.

The primary question is, how can the toxins, the evil, and wickedness be extricated from the hatred-addicted person? There is no chemical detox for hatred addiction. Hatred is a spiritual, mental, and emotional disorder. The addictive component of hatred is the dependent need to express and practice the unleashing of harmful expressions onto others.

In the process of expressing hatred, the mind, emotions, and body are employed. It is the autonomous self-will that dictate the execution of evil deeds through the cooperation of the mind, emotions, and behavior of the body. The hatred addiction toxins are spiritually connected to the mind and self-will. How can hatred be removed from the will and heart of the hater?

Public theology has answers for spiritual, mental, emotional, and behavioral illnesses. It is the purpose of this publication to heighten the awareness and the dangers of hatred addiction, and how hatred addiction can be understood, prevented, controlled, and treated. The publication, "God's Spiritual Prescriptions" offers Biblical and spiritual solutions.

Dynamics of Hatred and Drug Addiction

Hatred addiction is a self-induced compulsion to express harmful attitudes, thoughts and actions toward someone or some symbolic object to gratify an emotional release of anger or ill will. It is a means of ventilating negative feelings toward someone or symbolic personification who is disliked. Hatred addiction is characterized by deriving pleasure from a harmful act toward another person driven by a psychological pay off or emotional high or satisfaction.

Hatred is well known. However, it is not usually associated with addiction. Addiction is usually associated with the habitual use of drugs and dependence. Chemical addiction is sustained by continued use of the drug in light of knowing that the drug is harmful. Although the drug is harmful, the perceived benefits of euphoria, pleasure, relief from pain or state of wellbeing outweigh the harmful effects of the drugs. Similarly, hatred addiction persists due to the negative benefits of pleasure derived from hating others.

Hateful expressions are often used to relieve pain through ventilating stress and anger onto others. The hateful and harmful expression relieves tension from frustrations and anger. The hateful expressions may take the form of hateful words, violent or other detrimental actions against the hated person or personification. Hatred frequently leads to homicides, terroristic violence, and suicide.

Chemical addiction and hatred addiction cause psychological and neurological changes in the mind and the brain. Scientists estimate that the human brain has over one and a half billion brain cells. Chemicals and the intense emotional impact of hatred affect the neurotransmitters of the brain. The neurotransmitters of the brain are known as the "messengers" of the brain. They are the brain cells that transmit messages regarding feelings, thoughts and behaviors of the human body. These neurotransmitters can be significantly altered, impaired, damaged, or destroyed by chemical use and psychological abuse.

The brain is a sacred intricate fine-tuned organ of neurotransmitters. When these transmitters are impaired or damaged; feelings, thinking and actions can be significantly altered, distorted, exaggerated or dysfunctional. The healthy, fine-tuned brain keeps individuals connected to the reality of self, sanity, others and the world of reality.

Chemical addiction and hatred addiction are capable of distorting and obliviating the self and the world of reality. The dynamics of chemical and hatred addiction may not be generally known or understood. However, the news is replete daily, with voluminous senseless acts of crime and violence. Chemical damage to the brain and hatred to the mind are wreaking violence, wickedness, and high crimes against humanity hourly and daily. Chemical addiction and hatred addiction are not synonymous. Many persons who are addicted to alcohol and other drugs do not commit malicious crimes against others. However, the effects of the drugs impair their normal functioning. The primary difference between chemical addiction and hatred addiction is that hatred addiction is directed to other persons to do personal hurt and harm. Hatred addiction does not require an outside chemical component. The morbid hatred addiction is created within itself. The intake of chemicals may or may not be involved in hatred addiction. However, mood altering drugs can reinforce the effects of hatred addiction.

The nonhatred drug abuser can, and often does, use the drugs alone or in isolation from others. Therefore, the drug user is the primary victim of the drug. However, since drugs affect and impair judgment and work performance so severely, other persons are directly or indirectly affected. Alcohol and other drugs are doing great damage to the nation.

Hatred addiction in the 21st century poses a more serious threat than chemical addiction to humanity. Hatred addiction can be rational, methodical, and ideologically motivated for extensive pathological lethal and massive destruction. Hatred addiction is often expressed through hateful thoughts, emotional rage and ill will. It is expressed through monstrous frowns, evil eyes, obscene gestures, threatening words, conspiratorial manipulations, administrative intimidation, judicial demoralization, and even violent annihilation.

The chemically addicted person does not necessarily have to share his or her addiction with others. However, the very nature of hatred addiction requires the sharing of the pathological illness with others in order to get the euphoric high or psychological payoff. The serious down side of hatred addiction is that the addicted hater becomes an instrument to spread the toxic pathology to others. Hatred addiction is a contagion that spreads its influence through a variety of methods of examples and influence. It is characterized by being selfish, irrational, insidious, controlling, and intolerant.

The technology of social media has made it possible to spread hatred over the entire earth in very short periods of time. The new technology of mass communication has made it possible to saturate the community, the minds and nations with hatred that is unparallel in history.

This spread of hatred aided by information technology, is one of the greatest challenges for people of good will. The people of good will and faith in God must get involved in spreading the truth, good will, peace, and love through the mass media as never before. The battle of ideas, ideologies and spiritual warfare are escalating. The true believers must engage.

Hatred Terminologies

The oldest names and terminologies for hatred are found and referenced in the Bible over 210 times. The words used to describe hatred in the Bible are different from the words used to describe hatred in psychiatry and other health professionals. The Bible uses such words as wicked, evil, injustice, hypocritical, rebellious and abomination. Whereas, the psychiatrist, psychologist and other scientific health professionals use such terminologies as maladaptive behavior, antisocial, neurotic, psychotic, dysphoric, dissociative, homicidal, and suicidal. Drug abuse, dependence and addiction are used in the scientific lexicon.

The scientific terminology for hatred and the Biblical terminology for hatred do not contradict or invalidate each other. They are complementary and supplementary to each other. However, they are not always synonymous with each other. Hatred is a theological terminology. Addiction is a scientific terminology. Hatred addiction is used in this work to connect the science and the theology. Public theology embraces true science, true art, just law and true religion. This publication of Hatred Addiction and Recovery incorporates science, art, law and theology.

Biblical knowledge is the oldest and most authoritative knowledge regarding hatred and love. Hatred and love are central themes throughout the Bible. The Bible not only tells the story about good and evil in the world; but it also demonstrates the work of evil and good in the recorded historical events of the Bible. The message of the Bible is so significant for all individuals and nations, that to ignore it, invites cataclysmic perils and disasters.

The Bible is the greatest classical literature known to mankind. In proportion to its significance, it is abysmally neglected. Hopefully, the Bible museum that opened in Washington, D.C. in November 2017, will increase the study and knowledge of the Bible. There is no other book that rivals the relevance, wisdom, knowledge, and significance of the Bible. It is the spiritual GPS. It is the global moral compass for all people. The Bible is the greatest book on morality, ethics, spirituality, law, love, art, life, justice, righteousness, love, salvation, and the revelation of God in history.

The symptoms of hatred addiction and drug addiction may overlap with each other. They may also complement each other in the performance of harmful effects and harmful behavior. Drugs can impair the functioning of the brain. Hatred can also impair the functioning of the brain.

It is not uncommon for persons in the heat of passion to commit violent crimes. There are pleas in courts of "insanity," or "temporary insanity," for certain violent behavior or crimes that do not involve the influence of chemicals. Hatred without drug use or abuse can trigger rational or irrational damaging behavior.

Many violent crimes and terroristic crimes have been meticulously planned and executed with rational thought precision. In such cases, the brain functioned well. Because of this well-planned rational precision in the commission of a crime, the plea of mental illness or insanity is rejected by the court. However, there is a human criminal problem. The problem is the pathological ill will. It is this ill will that falls into the category of immoral unethical and spiritual illness or spiritual disorder. Hatred addiction can stand alone without the influence of drugs.

The Human Spiritual Capacity

Human beings have a spiritual capacity as a primary component of their being and personality. The spiritual capacity accommodates spiritual values such as morality, ethics, righteousness, justice, equality, and love. These are human foundational values for equitable social relationships and for civilized living in society. It must be noted that spiritual values preceded scientific values. Science and technology are relatively new in history. It must also be noted that true spirituality (religion) and science can coexist harmoniously.

The growing problematic dilemma and tragedy of the 21st century in America, is the gross neglect of man's spiritual domain capacity for enlightenment and education. Although public education in America was an outgrowth from the Judeo-Christian Church; public education, including the colleges and universities are moving away from the church and religion. The doctrine of separation of church and state, the outlawing of prayers and Bible reading in public schools, have further exacerbated the alienation of the church and public education. Therefore, the spiritual capacity of children are being detrimentally, grossly neglected.

Public education major in three domains of learning. The cognitive (intellectual) domain is the primary emphasis of public education. The affective (emotional) domain and the psychomotor (behavioral) domains to lesser extent. Within these three domains of learning, the emphases now are on STEM (Science, Technology, Engineering, Math) and sometimes art is included in STEAM. These educational and learning domains of public education, effectively diminishes the spiritual domain of learning in the public schools. This has the net effect of ignoring the spiritual domain of learning. The publication (The Way Out of Darkness) states, "It is unwise, irresponsible and dangerous to educate minds and ignore the ethical, moral and spiritual guidance of those minds." These neglected and empty spiritual capacities are being filled with alien moralities and evil spirits.

The spiritual domain of learning is foundational for all other knowledge and education. To neglect the moral, ethical and spiritual domain of our children is worse than criminal negligence. This ongoing negligence reduces our children's opportunity to find their true identity, purpose for living and connection with God. As I write this information on February 14,2018, the news media reports that a 19-year-old youth in Parkland, Florida, has shot and killed 17 people at the local school.

The growing hatred addiction in the American society is not a mystery. The moral, ethical, and spiritual capacities provided by God are being neglected and deprived of the Word, the way, the truth, and the life and the love of God. These precious capacities for love are being allowed and facilitated to be filled with hatred. This hatred flourishes and increases its contagion in a culture that embraces hatred and secularism instead of love and God.

Hatred as Addiction

Hatred as an addiction feeds on jealousy, envy and resentment to get an emotional high to feel good through inflicting pain on others. Expressions of hatred are accompanied with pathological pleasure. It thrives on taking away the values of others and the imposition of pain and suffering on them for sick pleasure and excitement. Hatred addiction represents the devouring of innocence to feed the wicked appetite of evil. It is mental, emotional, and spiritual wickedness.

Individuals addicted to hatred have a pathological need to utterly dehumanize another person or groups of persons. This is manifested by disrespect, demeaning and disregard. Hatred is motivated to inflict pain and suffering, deprivation, and death. It must not be ignored.

Some Motivations for Hatred Addiction

1. The abandonment of traditional family values to accommodate self-centered and selfish life styles.
2. The proliferation of anti-God, anti-Bible and anti-Christ sentiments to ignore truth, Justice, righteousness and unaccountability to God.
3. The elimination of the moral compass in government and society to accommodate arbitrary decisions, personal favoritism and unaccountability.
4. The dismantling of government merit systems to accommodate self-promotion, abuse of authority, arbitrary decisions, violation of due process and unaccountability.
5. Political corruption of judicial system to deny equal justice under the law and promote injustice and discriminatory and arbitrary public policy.

6. Political corruption of judicial system to deny equal justice under the law and promote injustice and discriminatory and arbitrary public policy.
7. The political corruption of public education for personal profit, special interest through creating an educational industrial complex for personal profit through privatization.
8. The weaponizing of government agencies to selectively damage and violate human and Civil Rights for greed and control through the abuse of authority and U.S. Constitution.
9. The vicious use of public office with public funds to damage innocent citizens through injustice of violating their rights, denial of due process of law to express their hatred.
10. Unreasonable delays and denials of due process of law for grievance hearings, Administrative hearings and judicial hearings to deny justice arbitrarily and capriciously out of hatred.
11. The sacrifice of truth, democracy, U.S. Constitution, Biblical mandates to deny justice because of selfish pride and misguided hatred.
12. The denial of truth, justice, righteousness, Biblical knowledge, sound doctrines and the spiritual domain of love and compassion to children in the schools systems, in order to perpetuate and sustain personal hatred addiction.

Core Nature of Hatred Addiction

Hatred addiction is an artificially induced ill will dependence and practice through the expression of detrimental pain and suffering on others for pathological benefits, satisfaction, and pleasure. It is artificial because it is not natural. It is based on injustice and ill will. Hatred is an antagonistic and destructive force against the sacred values of human life, and life itself. It seeks to extinguish life and self-destruct itself. The pathology is revealed through the ultimate satisfaction and exhilaration the addicted hater experiences when accomplishing his goal of inflicting pain, suffering and death.

Hatred addiction is manifested through hating enemies more than loving friends. Hatred addiction loves hatred and death more than love and life. Somehow, the addicted hater gets more pleasure out of hating than loving. This pleasure and satisfaction derived from hating is at the core of hatred addiction. This pleasure aspect strengthens and reinforces hatred addiction. This pleasure aspects of hating explains why hatred persists in spite of known damage, cost, and pain. As hatred addiction progresses, it becomes clear that the cost of the addiction far exceeds the benefits in reality. This is true in drug addiction and hatred addiction. Addicted persons to drugs and hatred risk their health, reputation, friendships, freedom, opportunities, mental health, safety, security, their lives, and the lives of others to satisfy their addiction.

Hating is sick excitement at the expense of others. It thrives on taking away values of others, including the joy and life of others. When hating becomes an addictive pleasure, the absence of hating becomes boredom, irritation and pain. This artificially induced drive becomes strengthened through practice and habituation. The morbid practice becomes needed for pleasure and satisfaction. There is a pleasurable pay off by hateful thinking, expressions, and actions. As an addiction hatred grows and becomes impulsively controlling. It becomes a morbid condition within itself. It gets into the mind the emotions and becomes spiritual wickedness that overrides the natural will of the addicted person. This self-perpetuating cycle of living to hate and hating to live is ultimate spiritual wickedness.

The theologians, psychiatrists, social scientists, addictionologists, educators, and judicial scholars must establish a priority of getting seriously and redemptively involved in this threatening hatred addiction epidemic. There is an urgent need for collaborative alliances to convene a comprehensive conference to study, plan, treat, control, prevent and extinguish hatred addiction throughout the earth, beginning in the United States of America.

There is every reason to be concerned. America and the world have never experienced hatred addiction of this magnitude and potential. Hatred addiction is contagious to vulnerable minds and people. Hatred has the unpredictable potential for spreading and influencing other individuals and groups. No particular group or persons are immune from hatred. Hatred is often irrational and insidious. Addictive behavior is known to impair judgment and violate legal, ethical, and moral values. Hatred is capable of inhabiting the minds, emotions, and hearts of all people, regardless of their race, ethnicity, nationality, age, sex, or educational level. No particular person or people are immune to hatred. Therefore, it can be concluded that hatred is a real (not imaginary) threat to all humanity.

Modern technology is the unique component that has exponentially increased the potential damage of hatred to catastrophic proportions by just one individual. One person or a few individuals are capable of committing massive murder and human damage unparalleled in human history with modern technological armaments. The astronomical advancement in modern technology to destroy human life is what is new in the 21st century. Technological capabilities in the hands of pathological hatred is an unpredictable lethal combination. Additionally, this contagion of hatred addiction is spread and transmitted through technological social media and cyber space. Lethal words, images, symbols, and ideologies can be and are transmitted through technology on a global scale. Hateful communications and transmissions are being spread by technological media.

To get some appreciable understanding of the seriousness and urgency of the growing hatred in American society, as well as other societies; one only needs to consider the large numbers of people who store negative, anti-social, hateful feelings and thoughts. These persons are seeking human targets and methodologies on who and how to unleash the stored, resentments, anger, and rage. This seething stored hatred is usually invisible until it erupts violently or lethally upon randomly selected unsuspecting, usually innocent, human targets.

Unfortunately, America is in this hatred addiction crisis and emergency because its' moral, ethical, and spiritual development did not keep pace with its scientific and technological development, and social and cultural impact. America and the world are caught up in a time horizon critical dilemma. That dilemma is to accelerate the internalization of ethical and moral values before the hateful misusers of technology destroy civilization.

Hatred is a toxic will and desire that poisons the mind, body, soul, and spirit individually and collectively. This hatred is contagious. It seeks to destroy truth, righteousness, love, life, and the values of life in rebellions against God. It is a serious monstrous wicked reality.

CHAPTER 8

The High Cost of Hatred

For what shall it profit a man, if he shall gain the whole world, and lose his own soul? (Mark 8:36)

And he said, This will I do: I will pull down my barns, and build greater, And there will I bestow all my fruits and my good......But God said unto him, Thou fool, this night thy soul shall be required of thee: Then who's shall those things be, which thou has provided? (Luke 12:18, 20)

For ye have turned judgment into gall, and the fruit of righteousness into hemlock. (Amos 6:12)

And in hell he lift up his eyes, being in torments, and seeth Abraham afar off, and Lazarus in his bosom. And he cried and said, Father Abraham, have mercy on me, and send Lazarus, that he may dip the tip of his finger in water, and cool my tongue; for I am tormented in this Flame. (Luke 16:23-24)

Let every soul be subject unto the higher powers. For there is no power but of God: the powers that be are ordained of God. (Romans 13:1)

The High Cost of Hatred

Hatred is a tragic squandering and waste of precious time, talent, resources, and life. It indulges and engages the most negative and base impulses and expressions of the human personality. It disrupts the chemical balance, rational reasoning, and responsible actions. Hatred has initiated countless irretrievable tragic actions. In fits of passionate jealous rage, countless victims have been assaulted, maimed, and murdered.

The news media is replete with acts of hatred, violence, and crime. Hatred seeks to kill, steal, and destroy (John 10:10). Revengeful attitudes of hatred focus on inflicting pain, suffering, and destruction. The hatred may be directed to property deprivation or property destruction. The behavior of hatred is designed to hurt and inflict pain and suffering. Perpetrators of hatred derive pleasure from the hateful behavior. The intensity of the hatred often determines the extent of damage.

In severe cases, mild expressions of hatred do not satisfy the desire for maximum expressed hostility. When small degrees of damage do not satisfy this intense desire to inflict pain, the hate perpetrator goes for the kill. He seeks to brutally inflict pain and blot out the inordinately despised life. Many commit serial murders and mass murders because the desires of insatiable hatred are so deep, intense, and entrenched.

Hatred addiction is similar to chemical addiction. Just as the chemically addicted person requires higher quantities of the chemical to get the desired effects, the hatred addicted person requires more intense expression of hatred to get the desired effect. In order to justify the pathological need to inflict suffering and death, the hatred addicted perpetrator becomes unreasonable and irrational in order to selectively disparage and discredit the values of human life. This is an indication where a person indulges in self-deception and creates his or her own separate reality. They will demonize innocent and even angelic people.

The high cost of hatred can readily be seen in these instances where the person filled with hatred, negates the values of life, the purpose of life and life itself. A simple cost benefit analysis of hatred indicates no benefits, but catastrophic losses. Hatred is an evil force against life. It has become an enemy to the benefits of life and life itself.

Weapons of massive destruction make the high cost of hatred unaffordable for humanity. It must be a top priority to rid the earth of hatred and evil. It can be done. Human beings are the haters. They were not born with hatred, and they were not born to hate. Hatred comes after birth from the social environment and surrounding culture. The things that breed hatred and reinforce hatred in the society can be identified and extricated, beginning with the proper care and education of children.

There is no excuse for anyone or humanity to perish for lack of knowledge at this late date in human history. The Prophet Hosea made the pronouncement that we "perish for lack of knowledge." This pronouncement was made in the 8th century before Christ. This was before most of the prophets were born. It was before the birth of Jesus and the New Testament. It was before the advent of science, electronics, motor vehicles or the printing press. Writing was crude and written documents were few and far between.

Primitive means of communicating and sharing knowledge two thousand eight hundred years ago give even more credence to the words of Hosea. At this present time in the 21st century, there is no excuse for being ignorant about God, the Bible, Jesus Christ, and the truth about the world around us. There is an explosion of knowledge, mass production and availability of Bibles and innumerate varieties of books. The telephone, smart phone, internet and social media provide constant access to all forms and variety of knowledge. There is no excuse to be ignorant in this 21st century. Most of the ignorance that we have in the 21st century is self-imposed.

The nature of hatred addiction rejects truth and knowledge to satisfy its pathological indulgence in the infliction of pain and suffering on others. The critical issue for the addictive hater is not the absence of knowledge or the unavailability of knowledge; it is the rejection of knowledge and truth. This is consistent with the gospel of John (John 1:11) "He came unto his own, and his own received him not." Therefore, it is not merely the lack of knowledge, it is the rejection of knowledge. The compulsion of addictive hatred is stronger than the desire for knowledge. The extremity of hatred is known to choose homicide and suicide rather than embrace life.

It would be redundant, superfluous, and impossible to document the daily ongoing overt and covert acts of hatred and human violence. Evil, wickedness, hatred, and violence against humanity are escalating daily. The costs of hatred have always exceeded the benefits. It has now reached the level of being unaffordable. This epidemic of destructive hatred is not sustainable. We have a choice to rid ourselves of this unsustainable hatred addiction epidemic. We also have a duty to God and humanity to love God and love each other.

The word of God is for human life. Jesus said that he came to "give life and give it more abundantly." Americans and people throughout the world have failed to make human life the top sacred priority that it is. To safeguard human life, more attention must be given to mental health.

Prioritizing Safeguards for Mental Health

The mental health of Americans is seriously and critically jeopardized. The daily news media is replete with the symptoms of mental disorders and emotional disturbances. Society is bombarded daily with horrendous reports of brutal crimes against persons, and property, and violations against unalienable human rights. There is an epidemic of identity thefts, hacking attacks, and drug abuse. The Atlanta Journal-

Constitution reported that thirty-three thousand persons died of opioid use-related deaths in 2015.

Many of our well-known colleges and universities are experiencing massive student disturbances, violence, and ideological confusion. Social media is saturated with raging ideological warfare, political dissension, sexual crimes, sexual confusion, unbridled greed, and unjustified expressions of hateful words and destructive deeds. Massive numbers of Americans are losing their mental health and spiritual hope, and dying silent unceremonious deaths. Mental and spiritual disorders are at the core of America's culture crisis. Basic American institutions are being corrupted with unsound doctrines, irrational ideologies, and social injustice. These imbalances create serious deficits in the human potential. These deficits degenerated into mental disorders, toxic relationships, and destructive behavior.

America must make mental health an urgent priority. The mental health of the head determines the health of the whole body. When the head is sick, the health of the whole body is jeopardized. Serious consideration must be given to the mental health status of all heads of organizations, especially those who head political, military, religious, educational, social, and economic organizations. Sick heads make sick groups, sick cities, sick states, and sick nations. Sick institutions make sick cultures. Mental and spiritual disorders have contagions that put every individual at risk. Dr. Martin Luther King, Jr. stated that "Injustice anywhere is a threat to justice everywhere." Mental and spiritual illness anywhere is a threat to mental health and life everywhere. Sickness is a prelude to death.

The protection and safeguards for the mind are lagging far behind the protection and safeguards for the body. Much of this is justified because the body houses the mind. The body is the temple of the spirit. Yes, the body must be well cared for. However, given the American and world culture crisis, it is urgent that priority be given to mind care and mental health maintenance and enhancement, beginning at birth, and continuing throughout life. The criminal and civil statutory laws are voluminous in protecting the physical body and even material property. However, laws designed to protect the mind, and the personal mental well-being of individual persons, are grossly inadequate and deficient. While there are many lawful and legal remedies to protect the body from threats, abuse, assaults, and violence, those legal protections are not in place for the protection of the mind and mental faculties. There are grossly too few legal protections and remedies to protect and safeguard the mind.

The following priorities from a theological and cultural perspective are recommended for restoring and maintaining optimum mental health for the people of God. Adopt legislation that will serve the cause of justice, peace, goodwill, equitable restoration, health, and prosperity in government and in society. Heeding the prophecy of Amos would be very helpful, "Let justice run down as water, and righteousness as a mighty stream." Require Biblical education and literacy in all public education. Establish impartial government merit systems based on equal education and employment opportunities. Establish fit-for-duty professional standards in all areas of government administration and service. Enforce and ensure public official accountability. Require conflict of interest disclosures for all legal representatives. Require the observance of explicit codes of professional ethics in all government and public service. Establish reasonable time limits for all grievance hearings and judicial litigation. Legislate and allocate the necessary money, resources, and personnel to provide the needed remedial, preventative, treatment, and growth services for at risk and afflicted persons with mental disorders according to the DSM-V (Diagnostic Statistical Manual of Mental Disorders) by APA (American Psychiatric Association). Include competent theological professionals along with other professionals who make public policy for the care of the mental and spiritual disordered persons.

PLEASE NOTE: THE MENTAL HEALTH CRISIS HAS ALREADY ADVANCED TO AN EMERGENCY IN AMERICA. IMMEDIATE AND DELIBERATE ACTIONS ARE REQUIRED!

Dr. Martin Luther King, Jr. was assassinated on April 4, 1968. He sacrificed his life for freedom and social justice. He left an enduring legacy of Civil Rights for the world. He made many profound statements. He made one in particular that we can expand and paraphrase. He said, "Injustice anywhere, is a threat to justice everywhere." In paraphrasing and expanding, we can say, "Evil anywhere, is a threat to goodness everywhere." "Hatred anywhere, is a threat to love everywhere." "Ignorance anywhere, is a threat to knowledge everywhere." "Oppression anywhere, is a threat to freedom everywhere." Violence anywhere, is a threat to peace and security everywhere." God has created one human family. The actions of one member affects the whole family. What side of the King legacy are we on? Some use Dr. King's name for personal gain and fame; and they participate in politics of blame and shame. The dichotomy of hatred must die so the dichotomy of love can live.

The Holy Bible
God's Special Revelation

The anti-God, anti-Bible and anti-Christ spirits are advocating taking the Bible out of public libraries. These anti-God spirits have long been advocating and demanding that Bibles be removed from hotel rooms and other public facilities. These anti-God and anti-human life spirits have declared open warfare on the Church and God's people. God's people and the Church of Christ must take a bold stand and repel the evil intentions and anti-God efforts of the anti-Christ spirits. These anti-God spirits do not have the right or authority to remove Bibles from libraries or any other public facility. The believers in Christ must stop caving in to the wicked wishes of the anti-God spirits. The earth is the Lord's and the fullness thereof, the world and they that dwell therein (Psalm 24). The Bible is God's Special Revelation of love and salvation to mankind. God's people must be diligent and courageous as never before to increase their efforts to distribute Bibles and teach the Word of God everywhere unceasingly. The Bible is our blueprint for life.

The Plan to Extinguish Hatred

Since hatred has many components, its extinction is multifaceted. The good news is that these components of hatred can be identified and isolated. The components of hatred are not mysterious. They are not new or uncommon to human nature. They have a long history associated with human nature since the beginning of mankind.

The hatred has been manifesting itself since the beginning of humankind dating back to Adam and Eve, the very first family. This hatred manifested itself in the Garden of Eden and resulted in the death of Abel by his brother Cain in the first family. This hatred is old. Where did it come from? What is the antidote to hatred? The antidote to hatred has always coexisted with mankind. This antidote to hatred has made it possible for humanity to maintain civilization into the 21st century. The 21st century has brought new components into the equation that threaten human survival. For the first time in human history there are new components that can exponentially increase the force and damage of hatred as never before.

The new component and lethal instrumental ally of Hatred is technology. The development of atomic, hydrogen and nuclear weapons in the twentieth century was a wakeup call to America and civilization. The use of atomic bombs in Hiroshima and Nagasaki in 1945 amplified the power of technology.

However, in 1945 America felt that it was morally and technologically in control of this awesome power of atomic and nuclear bombs. America also felt that it had the power to restrain the use of this technological power.

The technology continued to advance from the Second World War in 1945 through the Korean Conflict, the Civil Rights Movement, the Vietnam Conflict, the influx of immigrants, and the monumental increase of the TV, cell phone, and the internet through the turn of the century in 2000. It was in 2001, the infamous 911 when Middle Easterners hijacked four American commercial airplanes to fly into the World Trade Center in New York City and the Pentagon in Washington, D.C. The fourth plane crashed in Pennsylvania. Approximately 3000 people were killed in the World Trade Centers in Manhattan. This was a manifestation of radical Islamic terrorism against America. This precipitated wars in Afghanistan and Iraq under the George W. Bush administration. During the Obama administration ethnic identity politics gained momentum along with the LGBT movement and Black Lives Matter movement.

This growing social milieu of identity politics, cultural diversity, religious pluralism, and other heterogeneity provides more identity targets to single out to hate. The emphasis on national, religious, racial, and ethnic identity reinforces targets to hate rather than diverse human beings to embrace and love.

Hatred takes a great toll on mental health physical health, social health, and the well-being of society. It is so intent on its compulsion to hate, that it self-deceives to create false perceptions to justify its hatred toward innocent persons. Hatred distorts, exaggerates, and blurs reality. Hatred often self-imposes irrationality to reject reality to justify implementing its hate objectives. This compulsive embracing of ignorance, darkness, and irresponsibility, translates into evil, insanity, and a mental and spiritual disorder of monumental proportion. Hatred takes a great toll on humanity and civilization. In, this 21st century, hatred is getting too expensive to afford every day. It was hatred that falsely accused, unjustly arrested, unfairly tried, and violently crucified Jesus Christ on the Cross at Calvary. The crucifixion of Christ is God's perpetual revelation of the extremity, evil, and insanity of hatred.

Unaffordable Cost of Hatred

Hatred is a misuse and abuse of the mind, emotions, spirit, and self. It distorts, twists, and intoxicates the body and the personality. It is self-toxic and self-defeating. It can be spread through direct teaching, practice, and other influences. It is often detrimental and deadly in its effects.

It is irresponsible and frequently criminally negligent to allow hatred addiction to exist, spread, violate, and contaminate other persons and society itself. Hatred addiction is not given the priority for extinction as biological and bacteriological diseases.

When there are diseases of the body, especially those that reach epidemic proportions, the responsible healthcare professionals go to work seriously to contain, control, and eliminate the deadly epidemic diseases. They also put forth effort to warn the public of the hazards of the disease. Sometimes, they use quarantine to safeguard the public. They develop and use antitoxins and antibiotics as remedies to cure the disease. They go further and recommend ways and means to prevent the reoccurrence of the disease.

Bacteriological diseases can be managed more efficiently and predictably than mental, emotional, and spiritually-based diseases, for obvious reasons. The bacteria can be harmful to the tissues of the body but does not impact significantly on the behavior of the infected individual. Hatred is the primary influence of behavior due to its mental and emotional effects. Unlike the toxic and deteriorating effects of bacteriological microbes on the body, hatred often controls the feelings, actions, and behavior of the whole body.

Hatred addiction is a rational, emotion and spirit that possess and take over the whole body.

Considering the notorious harm and the unpredictable nature of hatred addiction, there is a serious duty of every responsible person to expose the unaffordable high cost of this lethal evil. It must be called out, identified, exposed, and targeted for extermination. It must be wiped out.

Hatred addiction is a capricious, unpredictable, transmittable dangerous mental, emotional, and spiritual disorder. Its goal and mission is to inflict suffering, pain, and death upon human life and the values of life. Human beings can no longer afford to be indifferent and in denial regarding this grave destruction of human life.

CHAPTER 9

Hatred Detoxification

Come unto me all ye that labor and are heavy laden, and I will give you rest. Take my yoke upon you and learn of me, for I am meek and lowly in heart, and ye shall find rest unto your souls. (Matthew 11:28)

And when he came to himself, he said, How many hired servants of my Father's have bread enough and to spare, and I perish with hunger! I will Arise and go to my father and will say to him, Father, I have sinned against Heaven, and before thee, and am no more worthy to be called thy son, make me as one of thy hired servants. (Luke 15:17-19)

Study to show thyself approved unto God a workman that needeth not to be ashamed, rightly dividing the word of truth. (2 Timothy 2:15)

Jesus answered and said unto her, whosoever drinketh of this water shall Thirst again; but whosoever drinketh of the water that I shall give him shall never thirst, but the water that I shall give him shall be in him a well of water springing up into everlasting life. (John 4:13-14)

Hatred Detoxification

The challenge of hatred detoxification is to extricate (remove) the hatred, salvage the hater and restore normal mental, emotional, and spiritual health. The toxic energy associated with hatred, damages the person who carries the hatred. It is said that hatred, "corrodes the vessel that carries it." How can hatred addiction be treated, arrested, withdrawn and the health of the addicted person be restored safely?

Medical healthcare through scientific methods and procedures have successfully defined how detoxification from chemical substances can be accomplished. It is important to be aware that the life of the chemically addicted person can be threatened unless the detoxification is done under competent medical supervision. Chemically addicted persons have been known to die when the drugs go out of their system without competent medical supervision. This accentuates that the body of the addicted person develops a dependence on the harmful (toxic) drug therefore the removal of the drug without proper detoxification can result in the death of the drug dependent person. It is a serious medical and health problem when the body develops the need to be maintained on a poisonous drug.

In many instances, the hatred addicted person, has developed a pathological need and dependence on hating. Hating has become a need for their psychological distorted mental and emotional equilibrium. They find a kind of comfort in chaos, satisfaction in confusion and exhilaration in the infliction of pain and suffering. They find pleasure in fighting and violence - not in love, peace, and harmony. This makes hatred addiction detoxification more complex than chemical addiction detoxification. Many addictive chemicals will naturally be eliminated safely from the body in a time period of days and weeks. Hatred does not eliminate from the body through the natural elimination process. It can be maintained indefinitely.

Hatred is not a chemical substance that can be flushed out of the system or neutralized by the injection or intake of another chemical substance. Hatred consists of negative thoughts, ill will and emotional rage against persons or objects severely disliked and resented. Therefore, the detoxification from hatred addiction requires multifaceted therapies involving the whole personality of the hatred addicted person.

The therapeutic detoxification treatment model for hatred addiction requires the involvement of the four domains of human learning - cognitive for the intellect, affective domain for the emotions, psychomotor for behavior and spiritual domain for the ethical, moral and theological considerations.

These four domains of learning accommodate the four foundations for operational sound doctrines. The four principles or foundations for testing and validating truth, are science, art, law (justice, and Biblical theology. These principles and foundations equip the public theological practitioner with the necessary resources to facilitate hatred addiction detoxification based on validated knowledge and sound true doctrines.

The detoxification process of eliminating hatred addiction can take days, weeks, months or even years. There are some rare instances where individuals have experienced religious conversion and ceased their hatred addiction and become loving persons. Such rapid regeneration and transformation represent a spiritual miracle. The traditional methods of educational, counseling, pastoral care and other restorative behavioral therapies require a longer period of time.

Some Elements of Hatred Addiction

Hatred addiction is the form of hatred that compels the individual hater to hate due to a gratifying dependence or need to hate to experience the gratification. Most individuals experience episodic isolated dislikes and resentments towards others. However, the episodic resentment or indignation goes away without any need to possess or obsess on the unpleasant experience. This kind of episodic hatred goes away without vestigial remnants.

Similarly, individuals use alcohol and other drugs occasionally without being addicted to the drug. They do have compulsive needs to continue using the drug out of cravings and compulsion. There is a difference between drug use and drug addiction. There is a difference between hateful expressions and hatred addiction. One is occasional use, and the other is a chronic condition.

Hatred addiction is based on negative, prejudicial stereotypical teachings and influence without true or valid knowledge. Hatred addiction is based on fictional scripted narratives to justify cherished false beliefs. Hatred addiction contrives and believes preconceived notions and judgments without facts or knowledge to justify a wishful desired belief. Hatred addiction sees what it wants to see, here's what it wants to hear to confirm what it wants to believe without the benefit of reality and truth.

In summary, hatred addiction is the manipulation of the presumptuous brain to distort, exaggerate and deny reality in order to achieve an inordinate desire and need for self-deception. This inordinate addictive hatred overrides reality, truth, and the brain. It withdraws from the common reality of the universe and creates a perceived reality of its own. In this perceived abstracted reality of its own, the inordinate need to hate, negates the significance of love and life.

The elements of hatred addiction must be a wakeup call for a massive program for hatred addiction detoxification and restoration for mental and spiritual health. America needs brain health, mental health, spiritual health, economic health, social health, political health and cultural health. These growing illnesses are serious threats to the nation and world.

Theological Guides for Healing Hatred Addiction

1. Make a commitment to love God, yourself and neighbor through benevolent associations and human services according to the word of God.
2. Adopt a successful personal identity, a significant life purpose, noble goals and spiritual empowerment to the glory of God.
3. Internalize in the heart, the mind, the soul and spirit, the eternal values of love, truth, goodness and beauty to the glory of God.
4. Focus time, energy and resources on creative and positive endeavors that serve Humankind and glorify God.
5. Make it a continuing priority to discover, realize, develop and actualize your God given gifts, talents and potentials for human services and blessings to the glory of God.
6. Become a vessel of true knowledge, hope, motivation and inspiration for human reformation and transformation according to the word of God.
7. Study the Bible to become the moral compass and theological guide for the knowledge of truth, the ways of justice, righteousness and peace according to the word of God.

8. Build on a solid foundation to support, protect, develop, sustain and share the precious values of life and glorify God.

9. Envision, dream and create virtuous ways and means to enrich, refine and sustain the gift and quality of human life through God inspired art, music and human services to the glory of God.

10. Be a goodwill ambassador: sow seeds of truth, kindness, encouragement, affirmation and love as you meet, greet and associate with others to the glory of God.

11. Create future oriented ideas and projects to develop and utilize your gifts, talents and potentials as a productive humanitarian contributor and servant to humanity to the glory of God.

12. Attend spiritual growth fellowship groups to find faith, grow faith, share faith and apply faith to edify sisters and brothers and to glorify God.

W. J. Webb, Addiction Theologist

Treatment Approaches for Addictive Illnesses

1. Evaluation/Diagnosis/Assessment
2. Inpatient Detoxification
3. Ambulatory Detoxification
4. Abstinence (Cessation of Use)

5. Chemotherapy
6. Detoxification Therapeutic Counseling
7. Individual/Group Therapy
8. Activity Therapy
9. Alcohol and Other Drug Education
10. Spiritual Support Groups (Including Twelve Steps)
11. Self-help Groups (AA, NA, Al-anon)
12. Case Management Services

The effective recovery process for the addicted client requires a therapeutic community and the creation of support systems.

W.J. Webb, MDiv, CAC II, CCS

From Addiction and Darkness to Spiritual Light Prerequisites For Spiritual Healing & Wholeness

The journey to spiritual healing and wholeness requires the following conditions and avenues of expressions:

- Something Noble and Significant to Believe in.
- A validated truth that is dependable and trustworthy.
- A value of significance that offers hope and is worthy of Embracing.

- A High Calling from God that merits Unconditional surrender and ultimate allegiance.

Prescriptions For Healing and Recovery

The prescriptions for Healing and Recovery require certain conditions, attitudes, and actions. The following is a general sequence of attitudes, conditions, and actions for the journey to Spiritual Healing and Wholeness:

1. An enlightened personal awareness and self-discovery.
2. An informed social and environmental awareness of the world of reality.
3. Enlightened personal, situational, and circumstantial awareness.
4. A self-searching personal reflection and introspection.
5. A reverent acknowledgement of reality, the love and the power of God.
6. An analytical and prayerful exploration of options and directions to fruition, recovery, and fulfillment.
7. Institute a comprehensive assessment of resources and support systems.
8. Adopt internal resolutions with mental and spiritual preparations.
9. Initiate an act of repentance and forgiveness of self and others.

10. Initiate liberating activities from the bondage of the past.

11. Embrace the survival values for successful and triumphant living.

12. Claim a personal spiritual identity rooted in the Word, Ways and Will of God.

13. Receive the infusion of faith, hope, love, truth and courage through study, prayer, meditation, worship and fellowship.

14. Continue to seek truth, knowledge, wisdom, understanding and their redemptive application in the will of God.

15. Identify and pursue specific missions, causes and purposes for living a meaningful abundant life for self and others.

16. Establish specific redemptive and salvation goals to edify humanity and glorify God.

17. Establish a dedicated focus on the mission, methods, and goals to be accomplished.

18. Develop a resolute and unwavering commitment to the cause and the high calling of God of which you have been commissioned.

19. Make investments for personal, intellectual, spiritual, educational and economic growth for uplifting humanity and for future returns.

20. Pursue goals of self-actualization, social redemption and human salvation.

The pursuit of spiritual healing and wholeness is a continuous process. It must become a way of life. The above prerequisites and prescriptions for healing and recovery must be inculcated in our pattern of living and the core of our being.

W.J. Webb, MDiv, MS, MA, CAC II, CCS

Pastoral Counselor, Public Theologian

References:

God's Spiritual Prescriptions for Healing, Liberation and Salvation. By Willie James Webb

The Way Out of Darkness: Vital Public Theology. By Willie James Webb

Core Values of America

These core values have served America well. They have made America the most prosperous and the most powerful country on earth. These values have afforded the citizens and inhabitants of America more freedom and opportunities than any other country on earth. These values must be asserted by all people of goodwill who value freedom and God's gift of human life:

1. One Nation under God.

2. Judeo-Christian Holy Bible.
3. The Declaration of Independence.
4. Representative government by the people, for the people and of the people.
5. The Church of Christ.
6. The common language of English.
7. The Apostles' Creed.
8. The United States Constitution.
9. U.S. Motto - "In God We Trust."
10. The Pledge of Allegiance.
11. Individual freedom.
12. Freedom of speech, religion, press, assembly.
13. Due process of law for life, liberty and property.
14. The equal protection of the law.
15. Self defense.
16. Freedom from unreasonable searches and seizures.
17. Respect for the dignity and sacredness of human life.
18. Freedom from involuntary servitude.
19. The institution of family and marriage between a man and a woman.
20. Compulsory school attendance for children.
21. Equal education and equal employment opportunities.
22. The free enterprise system.
23. Separation of governmental powers - Executive, Legislative, and Judicial.
24. Redress of grievances.

This is not intended to be an exhaustive list of core American values. However, it is important for every American to be knowledgeable of their core values to appreciate the historical sacrifices and the importance of their perpetuation for generations to come. (Christian Institute of Public Theology)

Biblical Ethical Authority
(The Christian Institute of Public Theology)

Jesus said unto him, Thou shalt love the Lord thy God with all thy heart, and with all thy soul, and with all thy mind. This is the first and great commandment. And the second is like unto it, Thou shalt love thy neighbor as thyself. On these two commandments hang all the law and the prophets. (Matthe 22:37-40)

How to be Ethical

Render therefore to all their dues: tribute to whom tribute is due; custom to whom custom; fear to whom fear; honor to whom honor. (Romans 13:7)

Owe no man anything, but to love one another; for he that loveth another hath fulfilled the law. (Romans 13:8)

Rationale for Discording Evil

And if thy right eye offend thee, pluck it out, and cast it from thee: for it is profitable for thee that one of thy members should perish, and not that thy whole body should be cast into hell. (Matthew 5:29)

And if thy right hand offend thee, cut it off, and cast it from thee: for it is profitable for thee that one of thy members should perish, and not thy whole body should be cast into hell. (Matthew 5:30)

Wherefore if thy hand or thy foot offend thee, cut them of, and cast them from thee: it is better for thee to enter into life halt or maimed, rather than having two hands or two feet to be cast into everlasting fire. (Matthew 18:8)

Offensive and Defensive Armor of God

Finally, my brethren, be strong in the Lord, and in the power of his might. Put on the whole armor of God, that you may be able to stand against the wiles of the devil. (Ephesians 6:10-11)

The Christian Institute of Public Theology, INC
Atlanta, GA

CHAPTER 10

Prescriptions for Healing

I will put my laws into their mind, and write them in their hearts: and I Will be to them a God, and they shall be to me a people. (Hebrews 8:10)

Create in me a clean heart, O God; and renew a right spirit within me. (Psalm 51:10)

Be not conformed to this world, but be ye transformed by the renewing Of your mind. (Romans 12:2)

He has sent me to heal the brokenhearted, to preach deliverance to the captives, and recovering of sight to the blind, to set at liberty to them that are bruised. (Luke 4:18)

Prescriptions for Healing

Knowledge Needed for Hatred Healing

Individual human beings are not born haters. Hatred is taught, learned, and acquired from the social cultural environment. Cultural is inclusive of all manmade things in the environment. It includes values, experiences, and influences in the living environment. Hatred is a mental and spiritual disorder (Ezekiel Saw the Wheel). It is a malevolence (sickness) of spirits acquired from the social and cultural environment. It is important to understand the pathological perspective of hatred in order to plan and effect a resolution of treatment and healing.

When hatred is viewed as an illness, this aids in objectivity and nonjudgmental attitudes towards the person harboring the hatred. There is a tendency on the part of many persons to judge or prejudge haters in a hostile and negative manner. There is also a tendency to hate haters or join them in their hating. When hatred is seen as an illness, it is easier to separate the hater from his or her illness of hatred. This makes it possible to extricate the illness of hatred and restore the person to spiritual and mental health.

Human beings can be transformed, changed, and converted according to the Gospel of Christ. Where there is life, there is hope, love and the possibility of repentance through faith, grace and the mercy of God. Paul persecuted the Christians (Acts 8:1-3). However, Paul was converted and became one of the greatest witnesses of the Christian faith (Acts 9:1-31).

Hatred addiction can be prevented, treated, and cured. If children were reared in the proper nurture and admonition of God, they would not become haters. Proverbs says, "Raise up a child in the way he should go, and when he is old, it will not depart from him." " It is possible to get rid of the hate nature, be born again (John 3:7), and become a new creature (2 Corinthians 5:17) in Christ.

The social and health histories of many haters provide credible information as to how and why the haters become haters. Hatred, although not justified, is a product of social and cultural conditioning and learning. Cultural, social, and environmental conditions contribute to the making of persons who hate. Societies play a role in creating individuals and groups who hate.

Hatred is far from being an isolated individual phenomenon. Therefore, it is essential to look beyond the individual hater in order to understand hatred and what can be done to prevent it, treat it and eliminate it. The individual's personal growth, development, learning and living experiences must be explored and studied in order to understand the affliction of hatred addiction. The lone hater is not always the individual who is totally responsible for his or her expressed hatred. Other social, cultural, and environmental influences contribute to hatred addiction.

The foregoing background on factors that contribute to hatred is provided in order to understand a regimen of healing for hatred addiction. Specific things to treat individuals afflicted with hatred can be done. However, since hatred is influenced by so many external environmental factors, these recommendations for treatment and healing of hatred will include the social, educational, cultural, spiritual and theological institutions and agencies. The treatment and healing of hatred addiction must be inclusive of the total cultural, political, economic, educational, religious, and governmental institutions and agencies.

The seemingly disjointedness of all of these agencies and institutions will be unified and undergirded by public theology. Theology provides the holistic meaning and purpose for human life in relation to the world and God. Human beings under God and through public theology have the responsibility for individual self-healing and healing of corporate humanity. Sick individuals contaminate and infect humanity with their sickness. Likewise, humanity spreads its illness to individuals. Spiritual illnesses and spiritual healing involve the individual and the group.

The introduction of public theology as a primary source of therapeutic healing for hatred requires some preliminary education and knowledge about biblically-based theology. It is unfortunate that many people in the American society are biblically and theologically illiterate and deficient. Individuals who sustain theological knowledge deficiencies are vulnerable for hatred addiction. It is the lack of theological knowledge that causes people to self-destruct and perish.

Many people, and especially those who are chronically addicted to hatred, are spiritually lost in the "Grand Scheme" of the universe. They are alienated from self, others and the purpose of life. God provides theological knowledge for humans to learn who they are and their purpose for living.

It is the duty of every person born into the world, to find his or her identity and purpose in life. Theology provides the foundations for making those vital discoveries. However, many people do not learn about theology in their homes. Many people do not have regular church attendance. Most American public schools prohibit the teaching of the Bible and theology in the public schools. The deprivation of this knowledge prevents many from learning their proper personal identification and purpose in life.

The following theological perspective will be helpful in providing an overview of questions regarding the foundations for true religion, the nature of God, God's authority, the unique Biblical word, the Gospel of Christ, the power of God to heal and forgive.

The Unique Biblical Word
The Christian Institute of Public Theology

The Bible is the incomparable unique book in the annals of human history. It is the only known comprehensive book that demonstrates in history the revelation of God's participatory intervention and actions to save humankind. It is the only credible book that tells the complete human story in 66 books from Genesis through Revelation. It is the only sacred literature that provides for the structural content of holistic systematic theology. The Bible provides for Bibliology, the doctrine of Scripture; Theology, for the doctrine of God; Christology, for the doctrine of Christ; Pneumatology, for the doctrine of the Holy Spirit; Anthropology, for the doctrine of man; Soteriology, for the doctrine of salvation; Ecclesiology, for the doctrine of the Church; Eschatology, for the doctrine of last things. These doctrines have evolved out of the context of historical living experiences of real people, at specific places, circumstances, and times. No other authentic historical literature can make these theological claims.

The Bible is its self-contained authority under God. The Bible is beyond the authority, the culture, and the statutory laws of man. The Bible is a unique collection of books that identifies and demonstrates the unique characterization of God. The Bible characterizes God as being omnipotent (all-powerful), omniscient (all-knowing), omnipresent (present everywhere at all times), infinite (without bounds), eternal (without beginning or end), immortal (not subject to death), Creator (creator of creation), redemptive Savior (eternal life for man through grace). God demonstrates through biblical history sound doctrines and values that are congruent with the following universal values and principles: Life made in the image of God; The reality of Truth; The enlightenment of Knowledge; The balance of Justice; The virtue of Goodness; The ways of Righteousness; The preciousness of Love; The art of Beauty; The Illumination of Light; The resilience of Hope; The perseverance of Faith; The understanding of Wisdom; The autonomy of Freedom. The essence of Human Nature. The Bible is the only book that describes what human nature is and what it does; in contrast with what human nature ought to be and what it ought to do according to the Will of God.

THE BIBLE CONTAINS THE WILL OF GOD. The Bible is the only credible book that reveals and demonstrates the continuity of God's Will for over 5000 years of documented revelatory human history on the earth. It is the only inclusive book for the whole person and for the whole world. It is the only known book that is based on the Will of God. The Bible is theologically guided by the WORD OF GOD. It is existentially EMPOWERED BY THE ANOINTMENT OF GOD. It is contextually engaged in the COMMISSION AND MISSION OF GOD. The Bible is prophetically proclaimed in the WITNESS OF GOD. It is strategically planned through the WISDOM OF GOD. It is systematically developed through the WAYS OF GOD. The Bible is holistically designed for the WORK OF GOD. THE BIBLE IS THE BOOK THAT INCLUDES AND SUBJECTS EVERY SOUL TO ITS JURISDICTION FOR THOSE WHO ARE LIVING, THOSE WHO ARE DEAD AND THOSE WHO ARE YET TO BE BORN.

THE HISTORICAL BIBLICAL ACCOUNT OF THE OLD AND NEW TESTAMENTS GAVE BIRTH TO JESUS CHRIST, THE SAVIOR OF THE WORLD. Jesus Christ is the most voluminously documented person of all history. More information is known about Jesus Christ and by more people than any other person of history. Jesus Christ is known through Old Testament prophecies, his celebrated birth (Christmas), his living events, miracles, crucifixion, resurrection, ascension, disciples, the gospels and 2000 years of innumerable witnesses. The gospel of Matthew (1:2-16) traces the genealogy of Jesus from Abraham to Jesus. The gospel of Luke traces the genealogy of Jesus back to Abraham, Adam, and God. Jesus Christ is more than just a historical figure. Jesus Christ is the only individual to become the global timeline of history. The advent of the birth of Christ caused the historical time keepers and the calendar makers to count backwards from his birth to the past and at the same time count forward from his birth to the future. Only Jesus Christ is the center of global history on the earth after two thousand years. The timeline of history is known as B. C. (Before Christ) and A. D. (Anno Domini, Latin, for, "In the year of our Lord"). The prophetic and messianic Scriptural references are too numerous to cite in this writing. However, to mention a few, the Gospel of John (1:14), "And the Word was made flesh, and dwelt among us," "He gave his only begotten Son (John 3:16),""I am the root and the offspring of David, (Rev. 22:16),""Neither is there salvation in any other: for there is none other name under heaven given among men whereby we must be saved. (Acts 4:12)." JESUS CHRIST IS THE BEST NEWS OF HISTORY. EVERYTHING HE SAID WAS GOOD NEWS. EVERYTHING HE DID WAS GOOD NEWS. EVERYTHING OTHERS SAID ABOUT HIM WAS GOOD NEWS. EVERYTHING OTHERS DID TO HIM WAS GOOD NEWS (EVEN THE SACRIFICIAL CRUCIFIXION).

THE WHOLE BIBLE IS GOD NEWS FROM GOD TO MAN AND ABOUT GOD FOR MAN. IT IS INSTRUCTIVE AND INCLUSIVE FOR EACH AND EVERY SOUL FOR ALL TIME AND ETERNITY. THE BIBLE TEACHES THAT GOD IS INESCAPABLE. THERE IS NO SUBSTITUTE FOR GOD, THE BIBLE OR THE ONLY BEGOTTEN SON, JESUS CHRIST. THERE IS ONLY ONE GOD WITH THE CAPITAL G. There are many idol, false gods with the small g.

Every individual must make it a top priority to learn the WORD OF GOD. We perish for lack of BIBLICAL KNOWLEDGE; BIBLICAL ILLITERACY IS TRAGICALLY DANGEROUS AND DESTRUCTIVE.

Massive minds have come to the conclusion that, 'No individual or group of individual artists, scientists, historians, jurisprudents, wise men, prophets, mystics or sages could create the Bible in a million years. ONLY GOD COULD BE THE ULTIMATE AUTHOR OF THE HOLY BIBLE!"

God Offers Healing for the Nations

Jesus Christ is the Whole Gospel for the whole person and for the whole world. Jesus offers healing for sick bodies, sick minds, sick souls, sick spirits, sick leaders, sick governments, sick religions, and sick nations. Never before in the history of the earth, has humanity witnessed such massive mental and spiritual disorders. The disobedience and rebellion against God is rampant in the society. These massive mental disorders and spiritual wickedness are happening at a time in history when man has the technological capabilities for unleashing weapons of mass destruction upon humanity. Mental and spiritual disorders combined with guns, bombs and nuclear weapons makes for a lethal threat to humanity.

Thanks be to God for sending the Savior in Jesus Christ. There is hope and healing in Jesus Christ. We must pray and trust God as never before. God's promises are still good. "If my people, which are called by my name, shall humble themselves, and pray, and seek my face, and turn from their wicked ways; then will I hear from heaven, and will forgive their sin, and will heal their land." (2 Chronicles 7:14)

God is Ultimate Authority and Absolute Power

God is the Creator of existence and all things, including human life (Genesis 1 & 2). Every soul is subject unto God (Romans 13:1). The Bible is the ultimate written authority over all human life. God has given and commanded universal divine and natural laws to govern the universe and the affairs of mankind. Mankind does not have the authority nor the right to alter or ignore the divine and natural laws of God. God blessed his creation and declared that it was very good. God declared in the gospel of Matthew, Mark, and Luke: "This is my beloved Son, in whom I am well pleased." God is pleased with the goodness of his creation, the truth of his Word and the Salvation of his Son. Therefore, when manmade laws go against the laws of God, they are invalid, unjust, confusing, chaotic and destructive, laws. "God is not the author of confusion."(1 Cor. 14:33). Valid laws must be just, righteous, and congruent with the divine and natural laws of God. Many manmade laws do not comply with the mandates of God. We must be reminded that the Bible has 192 references to fools and foolishness. Things are not created, blessed, and ordained by God's Word, do not uplift humanity, nor glorify God. The chief end of mankind is to praise and glorify God.

What is a True Religion?

A true religion is based on sound and true doctrines and practices that points to, and connects with, the will and reality of God. In true religion, God is recognized as being omnipotent, omniscient, omnipresent, infinite, eternal, immortal and Creator. The doctrines, principles and practice of true religion must be congruent and in harmony with the following universal values: LIFE, TRUTH, JUSTICE, GOODNESS, RIGHTEOUSNESS, LOVE, LIGHT, BEAUTY, FAITH AND HOPE. True religion is universally inclusive of all human beings as brothers and sisters under the Fatherhood of God. In true religion God is worshipped in truth and in spirit. True religion allows for the autonomy of the individuals free will as opposed to coercive intimidations of the mind and the involuntary servitude of the body. True religion contains redemptive revelations from God that are specifically manifested in a historical context of invincible evidence and infallible proof. Remember that religions, prophets, doctrines, and principles can be false. Therefore, it is vitally important for everyone to seek, ask, pray and study until you have found TRUE RELIGION THAT OFFERS SALVATION IN JESUS CHRIST.

Peace with God

There can be no outside peace without peace within. There can be no peace within without peace with God. The expressions of human conflicts, hatred, injustice, evil, bitterness, wars and destruction are outward manifestations of the rebellious and wicked hearts within. Evil minds and iniquitous hearts sow seeds of evil, confusion, and destruction. You cannot have true peace in your life, your home, your school, your church, your business, your society and nation until you have peace within from God. Faith in God through Jesus Christ is the top priority for peace and salvation for every human being. The Bible has 421 references to peace. "Therefore, being justified by faith, we have peace with God through our Lord Jesus Christ." (Romans 5:1) Let there be peace! Let it begin with me and you today!

The Creator, God, Owns Everything

The earth is not owned by any person, race, religious group, nationality or any designated people. Psalm 24:1 is explicit about the ownership of the earth and everything else. "THE EARTH IS THE LORD'S, AND THE FULNESS THEREOF; THE WORLD, AND THEY THAT DWELL THEREIN." (Psalm 24:1). It is a tragic sadness that there are human beings who think that they have the right or the authority to, "wipe," certain other human beings off the face of the earth or otherwise abuse, deprive and destroy them. The reprobate minds that think this way are sick with sin, in the gall of bitterness and spiritual wickedness. They are a curse to the earth and the wonderful blessings that God has created for mankind. Jesus Christ declared that he came to give life, and to give it more abundantly. The anti-Christ spirits and the anti-God spirits are determined to destroy human life and the goodness of the creation of God. The love, the resurrection, the grace and ascension of Jesus is a declaration that evil will not succeed. Every human being needs Jesus Christ as their Lord and Savior.

The Righteousness of God is the Standard

God has already set the standards for his righteousness for all mankind. It is perilous and dangerous to substitute the righteousness of man for the righteousness of God. Therefore, it is a primary responsibility for every person to learn the righteousness of God standards as set by God. This is vitally important because Proverbs 14:12 says, "There is a way which seemeth right unto a man, but the end thereof are the ways of death." Romans 10:2-3 confirms what Proverbs says in the following words, "For I bear them record that they have a zeal of God, but not according to knowledge. For they are being ignorant of God's righteousness, and going about to establish their own righteousness, have not submitted themselves unto the righteousness of God." Religious and political zeal without the righteousness of God and without the knowledge of God's Word, is perilous, deceptive and destructive. When people deviate from the ways of God, like sheep without a shepherd, they go astray. Judges 21:25 gives insight into self-righteousness in the following verse, "In those days there was no king in Israel: every man did that which was right in his own eyes." Thanks be to God for giving humanity a righteous king in Jesus Christ. Follow King Jesus, the Christ.

God Forgives and Heals

God wants his people to be healthy, whole and at peace with each other. However, all forms of sinfulness and sickness are raging in our world. Jesus Christ is the Great Physician. When he walked the earth, he demonstrated his ability to heal bodies, minds, spirits and souls. He resurrected some from the dead. He gave sight to the blind, hearing to the deaf and walking ability and agility to the lame. He healed persons with leprosy and those who were paralyzed. He cast out demons. He rescued a woman who was about to be stoned to death by a mob of unhealthy and misguided people. God and his Only Begotten Son Jesus Christ are still in the healing business. All individuals and nations need this healing: 2 Chronicles gives us God's requirement for forgiveness and healing: IF MY PEOPLE WHICH ARE CALLED BY MY NAME, SHALL HUMBLE THEMSELES, AND PRAY, AND SEEK MY FACE, AND TURN FROM THEIR WICKED WAYS; THEN WILL I HEAR FROM HEAVEN, AND WILL FORGIVE THEIR SIN,

AND WILL HEAL THEIR LAND (2 Chronicles 7:14). Let us begin individually to meet this requirement and pray that it spreads throughout the earth.

The GOOD NEWS that Requires Telling

JESUS CHRIST, the SAVIOR of the world, is the greatest news to ever come to the planet earth. Jesus comes with truth, eternal life, the way to God, spiritual light, light of the world, love, wisdom, knowledge, authority, healing, mercy and forgiveness. He came in the flesh as Mary's Baby. He was and is the Word that was made flesh (and dwelt among us), lived, grew, crucified on a cross, buried, resurrected, commissioned his disciples, and ascended to live forevermore. The additional good news is, that this truth is recorded in human history with invincible evidence and infallible proofs. It was the single event that split the history of the world into BC (Before Christ) and AD (In the year of our Lord). That is how and why we arrive at today's date. If you have heard and received this GOOD NEWS, you are required to go and share it with others. Go tell It On The Mountain. Tell it in the valleys. Tell the GOOD NEWS to family, colleagues, neighbors, friends and foes. Tell it to the churches, schools and every segment of the community. Tell it with your voice, pen and paper, by mail and email, the telephones, smart phones, the internet and social media, that JESUS CHRIST is come!

Twelve Steps to Recovery of AA

Alcoholic Anonymous is the foremost self-help program. It is internationally known and practiced. It is an effective model to provide treatment and sobriety maintenance for individuals addicted to alcohol. It grew out of the church of the Christian faith. NA (Narcotics Anonymous) is a derivative of AA (Alcoholics Anonymous). NA is a self-help and recovery fellowship group for individuals addicted to drugs, other than alcohol. The same principles of fellowship are used in AA and NA.

A hatred anonymous group would be very helpful in coping with the problems of hatred addiction. Fellowship groups that acknowledge God are very effective in restoring sobriety, sanity and productive and positive living.

Fellowship groups is a place where faith can be found; where faith can grow; where faith can be shared and where faith can be practiced. HA (hatred anonymous) groups are encouraged. The fellowship group is a place where illness can be healed; knowledge can be learned; darkness can be enlightened; doubt replaced with hope; hatred replaced with love; failure replaced with success in God.

A copy of the AA Twelve Steps is provided as a successful model for other self-help groups, and especially for hatred addiction.

God inspired fellowship groups can be therapeutic, healing and restorative of health and optimum positive human functioning. There are numerous names for such a healing and restoring fellowship group. The AA fellowship model is classic and has already proved its merit.

We are obligated as Americans and as human beings to eliminate hatred from the earth. Hosting healing fellowship groups is a significant beginning.

TWELVE STEPS TO RECOVERY
(Alcoholics Anonymous)

1. We admitted we were powerless over our addiction - that our lives had become unmanageable.
2. Came to believe that a power greater than us could restore us to sanity.
3. Made a decision to turn our will and our lives over to the care of God as we understood Him.
4. Made a searching and fearless moral inventory of ourselves.
5. Admitted to God, to ourselves, and to another human being, the exact nature of our wrong.
6. Were entirely ready to have God remove all these defects of character.
7. Humbly ask God to remove our shortcomings.
8. Made a list of all persons we had harmed and became willing to make amends to them all.
9. Made direct amends to such people wherever possible except when to do so would injure them or others.

10. Continued to take personal inventory and when we were wrong, promptly admitted it.
11. Sought through prayer and meditation to improve our conscious contact with God as we understood him, praying only for knowledge of His Will for us and the power to carry that out.
12. Having had a spiritual awakening as the results of these steps, we tried to carry this message to addicted people, and to practice these principles in all our affairs.

CHAPTER 11

Immunity to Hatred

A new commandment I give unto you, that you love one another; as I have loved you; that ye also love one another. (John 13:34)

Let this mind be in you that was also in Christ Jesus. (Philippians 2:5)

Brethren, I count not myself to have apprehended; but this one thing I do, forgetting those things which are behind, and reaching forth unto those things which are before, I press toward the mark for the prize of the high calling of God in Christ Jesus. (Philippians 3:13)

Finally, my brethren, be strong in the Lord, and in the power of his might, Put on the whole armor of God, that ye may be able to stand against the wiles of the devil. (Ephesians 6:10-11)

Immunity to Hatred

It has been established that a child is not born with hatred nor any other psychic qualities. Dr. Maria Montessori (The Absorbent Mind) contends that the newborn child is born only with, "constructive possibilities which determine his development, and this will take its characteristics from the world about him." The child receives his mental, emotional, social and spiritual development in conjunction with his interaction and absorption with the world around him. The existence and development of hatred can be studied.

This brief foundation provides a baseline to study and evaluate the things and influences in the environment that cause or contribute to the development of human values and how such an illness of hatred addiction is acquired. Since the mystery of hatred is ruled out; science, art, law and theology can provide an understanding of hatred sufficiently to understand it, eliminate it and prevent it.

Prioritizing Safeguards for Mental Health

The mental health of Americans is seriously and critically jeopardized. The daily news media is replete with the symptoms of mental disorders and emotional disturbances. Society is bombarded on a daily basis with horrendous reports of brutal crimes against persons, property and violations against unalienable human rights. There is an epidemic of identity thefts, hacking attacks and drug abuse. The Atlanta Journal Constitution reported that thirty-three thousand persons died of opioid use related deaths in 2015.

Many of our well-known colleges and universities are experiencing massive student disturbances, violence, and ideological confusion. Social media is saturated with raging ideological warfare, political dissension, sexual crimes, sexual confusion, unbridled greed and unjustified expressions of hateful words and destructive deeds. Massive numbers of Americans are losing their mental health and spiritual hope, and dying silent unceremonious deaths. Mental and spiritual disorders are at the core of America's culture crisis. Basic American institutions are being corrupted with unsound doctrines, irrational ideologies and social injustice. These imbalances create serious deficits in the human potential. These deficits degenerate into mental disorders, toxic relationships and destructive behavior.

America must make mental health an urgent priority. Mental health of the head determines the health of the whole body. When the head is sick, the health of the whole body is jeopardized. Serious consideration must be given to the mental health status of all heads of organizations, and especially those who head political, military, religious, educational, social and economic organizations. Sick heads make sick groups, sick cities, sick states and sick nations. Sick institutions make sick cultures. Mental and spiritual disorders have contagions that put every individual at risk. Dr. Martin Luther King, Jr. stated that, "Injustice anywhere is a threat to justice everywhere." Mental and spiritual illness anywhere is a threat to mental health and life everywhere. Sickness is a prelude to death.

The protection and safeguards for the mind are lagging far behind the protection and safeguards for the body. Much of this is justified because the body houses the mind. The body is the temple of the spirit. Yes, the body must be well cared for. However, in view of the American and world culture crisis, it is urgent that a priority be given to mind care and mental health maintenance and enhancement, beginning at birth and continuing throughout life. The criminal and civil statutory laws are voluminous in protecting the physical body and even material property. However, laws designed to protect the mind, the personal mental well-being of individual persons, are grossly inadequate and deficient. While there are many lawful and legal remedies to protect the body from threats, abuse, assaults and violence, those legal protections are not in place for the protection of the mind and mental faculties. There are grossly too few legal protections and remedies to protect and safeguard the mind.

The following priorities from a theological and cultural perspective are recommended for restoring and maintaining optimum mental health for the people of God. Adopt legislation that will serve the cause of justice, peace, goodwill, equitable restoration, health and prosperity in government and society. Heeding the prophecy of Amos would be very helpful, "Let justice run down as water, and righteousness as a mighty stream." Require Biblical education and literacy in all public education. Establish impartial government merit systems based on equal education and employment opportunities. Establish fit for duty professional standards in all areas of government administration and service. Enforce and insure public official accountability. Require conflict of interest disclosures for all representatives. Require the observance of explicit codes of professional ethics in all government and public service. Establish reasonable time limits for all grievance hearings and judicial litigation. Legislate and allocate the necessary money, resources and personnel to provide the needed remedial, preventive, treatment and growth services for the at risk and afflicted persons with mental disorders according to the DSM-V (Diagnostic Statistical Manual of Mental Disorders) by APA (American Psychiatric Association). Include competent theological professionals along with other professionals who make public policy for the care of the mental and spiritual disordered persons.

PLEASE NOTE: THE MENTAL HEALTH CRISIS HAS ALREADY ADVANCED TO AN EMERGENCY IN AMERICA. IMMEDIATE AND DELIBERATE ACTIONS ARE REQUIRED!

Take Good Care of Your Mind

The mind is an invaluable treasure in an earthen vessel. It is the seat of consciousness of self, others and the world around us. We must make it a top priority to take the best of care for our minds. A significant function of the mind is to see and perceive the world of reality through the eyes of God and with the mind of Christ. In order to do that we must not allow our minds to be trash and garbage collectors. It must not be a place where fear, envy and jealousy reside. It must not be a place of emptiness and idleness. The mind must not be a place to store negative thoughts and bad revengeful feeling's. It is the responsibility of each person to educate his or her mind with the ongoing Word of God, and with truth, knowledge, understanding, wisdom, goodness, beauty, faith, hope and love. We must take good care of our minds so that we can see, hear, feel, sense, think and clearly interpret God's magnificent creation and His wonderful world of reality and His Salvation in Jesus Christ.

Your Most Important Priority
Study the Word of God

God has sent a personal message to all the people of the earth. The message is plain. It is in a book known as The Bible. It is written in your language. It is an urgent message. Jeremiah 22:29, cries out, "O Earth, Earth, Earth, hear the Word of the Lord." Isaiah exclaims, "Hear O Heavens, and give ear, O Earth; for the LORD has spoken. "My Word that goes forth out of my mouth shall not return unto me void (Isaiah 55:11)." Luke 11:28 says, "Blessed are they that hear the Word of God, and keep it." God's Word in the Holy Bible and the Word that "became flesh and dwelt among us," in Jesus

Christ is the most important for every living soul. "Thy Word is a lamp unto my feet and a light unto my pathway (Psalm 119:105)." God's Word is "the Way, the Truth and the Life." God's Word is Light, Knowledge, Wisdom and Understanding. God's Word is our lifeline for Salvation. 2 Timothy 2:15, "Study to show thyself approved unto God, a workman that needeth not to be ashamed, rightly dividing the word of truth."

The Fatherhood of God

Jesus Christ personalizes God and connects God to humanity by addressing God as," "Our Father," "The Father" and "Father." Jesus, through love and grace connects God to and with the universal human family as the FATHER of all. God, in Jesus Christ, becomes the loving producer, provider, protector and Savior of mankind. Jesus is good news because he is God News - The ultimate news about God. Jesus is good news to the world through the Fatherhood of God. Jesus demonstrates through the good news of the Gospel that God is involved in the agonizing human struggle. The Heavenly Father sends his Only Begotten Son to partner with us in the building of his Kingdom on the earth and to bring salvation to all those who will believe and receive. It is the solemn duty of the earthly fathers and all men to take the leadership in majoring in the serious business of fatherhood and the responsible and Godly rearing of children. It is the solemn duty of every person to support and esteem manhood and fatherhood. The significant roles that men and fathers must carry out have been given and ordained of God. Let us teach all our children at an early age to say, "Our Father, which are in heaven, hallowed be thy name, thy kingdom come..."

The Matchless Love and Gifts of God

Consider the matchless gifts of God, and you will be humbled, gratified, and amazed. God gives your life through your mother and father. He gives you a human family and a place to live on the earth. He gives you air to breathe, water to drink, food to eat, clothing to wear, shelter to protect and an environmental support system to sustain life. God gives your eyes to see, ears to hear, nose to smell, skin to feel, a mind and a spirit to discern and behold the majestic, glorious wonders of the earth and the heavens. He gives you light and truth to direct your pathway. He gives you a self-will to choose that which is good, just and righteous. God gives you a spirit to relate to him and to your sisters and brothers. God gives you eternal life through Jesus Christ. God's giving is an expression of his infinite love for life and his omnipotent power to sustain life. God loves us so much that he gives us the capacity to witness the marvels and mysteries of existence and creation. God has made us witnesses of the bountiful earth, the hanging moon, the shining sun and the twinkling stars. How will you show your gratitude to God?

Be Grateful

God created the magnificent universe. He created living things - plant and animal life. God created you and me. He created us in his image and likeness. He gave us a mind to reason and to witness the marvels and mysteries of his unfathomable creation. He gave us a mind to think and to reason and a language to communicate with each other and with God. He gave us a heart to love God and to love one another. God gives us parents and families. God gives us food, water, clothing, and shelter to sustain our lives on the bountiful earth. God gives us the Bible - His Book of instructions for life and living. God gives us a Lord and Savior in Jesus Christ to give us abundant and eternal life. Be grateful to God for life and your life. "Glory to God in the highest, and on earth, peace, good will toward men (Luke 2:14)."

The Transforming Journey Through the Bible

An invitation is extended to every person to take Route Sixty-Six and take a mental, spiritual, and emotional journey through the Holy Bible from Genesis through Revelation. A serious, studious, and faithful journey through the Bible can transform your life into a new creation in Christ. For those who love truth and the Word of God, the journey through the Bible will be the most fascinating, exciting, rewarding, and transforming experience of your life. Each of the sixty-six books of the Bible is an insightful spiritual journey. Those who do not take this biblical journey will have missed out on God's Personal Love Letter of Revelation to them. They will have missed out of God's connection with mankind in history over a five-thousand-year period. Many people embark upon physical geographical journeys throughout America and other countries. They take ocean cruises, historical sightseeing, recreational resorts, beaches, carnivals and playland activities. These physical geographical journeys and recreational excursions can be refreshing and rewarding. However, we must take special care not to neglect our souls. The journey through the Bible is a journey for the soul and the abundant eternal life. It is a journey that teaches how to connect with God. ROUTE 66 WILL TAKE YOU TO THE WAY, TRUTH AND THE LIFE! LET US INCREASE OUR BIBLE JOURNEY GROUPS!

Immune System for Mental Health

The growing American culture of corruption and confusion jeopardizes the mental health of millions of American people. There is a marked decline in ethical, moral, spiritual, and biblical social values. The American society is becoming more secular, the exclusion of the knowledge of God. Christian education, biblical study, church attendance, and the witness of God in the public square are on the decline in American society. A spiritually impoverished culture turns away from the survival values of truth, justice, righteousness, and love.

Decisions are made by selfish, arbitrary and unreality-based methods. Such bad, unwise, and arbitrary decisions and actions create confusion, corruption, disorder, and destabilization in the minds and in the culture. Two Scriptural references can give us immunity against this mental confusion. "And be not conformed to this world: but be ye transformed by the renewing of your mind" (Romans 12:2). "Let this mind be in you, which was also in Christ Jesus" (Philippians 2:5). The mind of Jesus Christ has the power to keep your mind sane and sober from the corruption and confusion of this world and be transformed by the renewing of your mind.

Appeals to Aid Healing

Some people got hooked on hatred due to being victimized by the hatred of other persons and/or systems. They were victimized by injustice and never received the compensation or the vindication that justice requires. The haters who were victimized by hatred themselves carry a painful and heavy burden. They live with unrelieved pain and sorrows. So often, this pain will not disappear or go away on its own.

There are temptations to go out and get personal revenge against the persons and systems that victimized them. Many victimized people go out and take retribution into their own hands. Most of the time such revengeful actions create additional problems and pain. In such a moral dilemma, theological consultation is essential. Hebrews 10:30 says,

"Vengeance belongs unto me, I will recompense, saith the Lord." Romans 12:19 says, "Dearly beloved, avenge not yourselves, but rather give place unto wrath: for it is written, vengeance is mine; I will repay, saith the Lord." Psalm 37:1 says, "Fret not thyself because of evildoers, neither be thou envious against the workers of iniquity." Psalm 37:8 says,' "For evildoers shall be cut off."

Following this theological wisdom of God, allows the victims of hatred to remain positive, law abiding, loving and true to the Gospel of Christ. This theological approach enables the unrequited victim of hatred to remain rational, ethical, effective, and victorious in the fight against hatred and evil. Humane, responsible, and right-thinking people should always be in the fight against hatred and evil. However, when one becomes personally victimized by hatred and evil, this ought to be a wakeup call that a serious warfare is going on. Therefore, you must put on the whole armour of God.

The Apostle Paul gives the admonishment for the Christian fight in the following statement: "Finally, my brethren, be strong in the Lord, and in the power of his might. Put on the whole armour of God, that ye may be able to stand against the wiles of the devil. For we wrestle not against flesh and blood, but against principalities, against powers, against the rulers of the darkness of this world, against spiritual wickedness in high places (Ephesians 6:10-12)."

Since the ground work for Christian warfare has been established, public theological engagement provides an avenue for ministerial services and a positive fight against injustice. When God says vengeance belongs to him, it does not mean for God's people to be passive, idle and indifferent. God partners with his people to bring about righteousness and justice in the society.

For those who are eager to do evil for evil, it must be remembered, that it is not profitable to become evil in the fight against evil. Servants of God must be redemptive in their engagement with hatred and evil. Hatred and evil represent a squanderous destructive waste of God's gifts to mankind. Preserve the gifts.

The following information on public theological redemptive engagement is provided for civility and redemption in the pursuit of social justice:

Public Theology Redemptive Engagement

The public theological engagement is for ethical, moral, social and spiritual guidance. Science can teach us what is over a broad spectrum. However, scientific knowledge does not exhaust the meaning of things. True religion goes beyond the scientific what is and teaches us what ought to be. What ought to be is the Will of God. The Will of God has been expressed more completely in the Bible and Jesus Christ than any other known source. God is the ultimate authority and the ultimate source of power. If true success is to be achieved in the social arena of human life, the will of man (human kind) must be in congruence with the Will of God. Therefore, the will of our appeals must take into consideration the Will of God.

Foundations for Petitions and Appeals

The petitions and appeals of the clergy (others can be included) as engaging public theologians, must be biblically based in the Will of God; theologically guided by the Word of God; contextually engaged in the commission of God; prophetically proclaimed in the Witness of God. Systematically developed through the Ways of God; existentially empowered under the anointment of God; wholistically designed for the work of God. The observance of these foundations will provide the essential sound doctrine and legitimate authority for diligent actions and perseverance.

Instruments and Methods of Appeal

Petitions and appeals are more effective when they are written with specific requests, based on specific issues and undergirded by legitimate moral authority. The written petitions and appeals can be reinforced by personal appearance, vocal expressions, alliances, outside interventions, assemblies and demonstrations when deemed appropriate and effective. The petition and appeal must be directed and officially transmitted to the appropriate person or agency representative authorized to receive such petitions and appeals. A reasonable length of time for response must be stipulated in the written appeal or petition (within 10 days or 30 days from time of receipt or a specified date).

Grounds for Petitions and Appeals

Grounds and appeals cover a wide range of complaints, grievances, resolutions and other requests for attention, hearings, responses and resolutions. The list can be very long. It is a Method of communicating a dissatisfaction and a request for resolution or remedy without higher appeals or other interventions. Many complaints are resolved in this manner. The written appeal lay the ground work for the moral, ethical, or legal gravity of your complaint. It helps the individual or agency to decide expeditiously on the options and the cost of responding to the appellant. They are usually persuaded to give the appeal more serious attention when it is in writing.

1. 1.Individual, human and social injustice. The dysfunctionality of government.
2. Unlawful discrimination in education, employment, housing, public accommodations and technological inaccessibility.
3. Unethical, immoral, unlawful, illegal and criminal violations of law and person.

4. Human deprivations, environmental injustice, negligent and endangerment, community Hazards and nuisances.

5. Political misrepresentations, disparate treatment in voting precincts, disparate location of government services (outside of the inner city), arbitrary late payment fees and excessive reconnection utility charges.

6. Sacrilegious laws, actions, issues involving attempts to take Christ out of Christmas Songs, restricting Nativity Scenes, removing crosses that honor the war dead, disallowing legally approved elective courses of the Old and New Testament to be taught according to law in the high schools in Georgia. Etc.

7. The allowance of school systems that violate and demoralize teachers and provide inferior education to thousands of students and the superintendents and school boards are unaccountable.

Benefits of the Written Petition and Appeal

The written appeal and petition document the problem, issues, and violations and also provide a proposed recommendation for resolution. When the appeal is in writing it conveys a serious intent. It is a transmittable composite form of your complaint or appeal that does not require your presence, and therefore, saves you valuable time. It helps to exhaust administrative remedies and establishes a foundation for accelerated legal, political, community, news media, social media and other possible allied support services and exposures. It documents the basic facts and story of your concerns for future reference if needed.

Make Real Your Appeals
(Precisely Written)

1. ADDRESS, DIRECT AND TRANSMIT your appeal to the responsible, authoritative Person, agency, or institution in charge.
2. DESCRIBE WITH FACTS AND SPECIFICITY THE PROBLEM, injustice, inequity, damages, cost, negligence, deprivation, hardship, and other detrimental consequences of the problem.
3. Enumerate with clarity the designated appropriate professional, negligent, ethical, legal, civil and any other human rights violations with dates or approximate dates of their occurrence, place and circumstance. List witnesses and evidence.
4. REQUEST IN YOUR APPEAL THE SPECIFIC REMEDY, CORRECTION, SOLUTION, RESOLUTION, COMPENSATION, POLICY, LEGISLATION, REPARATION, OR WHATEVER CORRECTIVE ACTION IS REQUIRED TO SOLVE THE PROBLEM AND RESTORE WHOLENESS.

5. STIPULATE AND REQUEST in your appeal a reasonable time limit and date for response to your appeal to avoid the necessity for further actions.
6. THIS APPEAL MUST BE TRANSMITTED VIA CERTIFIED U.S. MAIL WITH RETURN RECEIPT OR A PERSONAL VERIFIABLE DELIVERY AND CONFIRMED RECEIPT.

The Body of Jesus Christ

The Church represents the Body of Jesus Christ. The Body of Jesus Christ is a Body of Love. The Body of Love is a fellowship of Believers who accommodate whosoever will let him or her come. In this Body of Love, there is room for repentance and forgiveness. There is room for goodness and mercy. There is room for justice and righteousness. There is room for joy and beauty. There is room for peace and goodwill. There is room for brotherhood and sisterhood. There is room for truth, knowledge, wisdom and understanding. There is room for meditation, prayer and worship. There is room for preaching and teaching the Gospel. There is room for serving our sisters and brothers to the glory of God. However, there is no room for hatred and wickedness in the Body of Christ and in the hearts and lives of God's people.

Immunity to hatred is accomplished when an individual accepts the new life in Christ and the servanthood to God, that allows no time, no interest, no resources and no desire for evil, hatred, wickedness and death. The new life in Christ is wedded to the eternal values of goodness, truth, hope, faith, beauty and love. The new life in Christ is the eternal light of life that has overcome death and darkness.

CHAPTER 12
Cultural Transformation

And thou shall love the Lord thy God with all thy heart, and with all thy soul, and with all thy mind, and with all thy strength: this is the first commandment. And the second is like, namely this, Thou shall love thy neighbor as thyself. (Mark 12:30)

Train up a child in the way he should go: and when he is old he will not depart from it. (Proverbs 22:6)

And God blessed them, and God said unto them, Be fruitful and multiply, and replenish the earth, and subdue it: and have dominion over the fish of the sea, and over the fowl of the air, and over every living thing that moves upon the earth. (Genesis 1:28)

These words which I commend thee this day, shall be in thine heart, and thou shall teach them diligently to thy children, and shall talk of them when thou sittest in thine house, and when thou walkest by the way, and when thou liest down, and when thou risest up. (Deuteronomy 6:6-7)

Guides for Cultural Transformation

1. **Reflection:** Assessment of cultural change, meditate on cultural conditions and options available for transformation.

2. **Repentance:** Confess genuine sorrow and guilt for years of neutrality, indifference missed opportunities, forfeitures, and failures.

3. **Forgiveness:** Petition God for forgiveness for neglecting the health of the family, the church, the community, the culture, the nation, and society.

4. **Fellowship:** Join spiritual group for unity, knowledge, understanding, wisdom, growth, support, direction, resources, and service.

5. **Theological/ Bible Study:** Regular study of the inspired Word of God and theological knowledge passed down through centuries for the ultimate salvation of humankind. It is knowledge beyond culture.

6. **Mind Renewal:** Embrace the Gospel enlightenment of Truth, the Light, the Way, Wisdom, Holy Spirit and the mind of Christ.

7. Rebirth: Conversion, regeneration, New Nature,
                        New Creature, rededication, new
                        resolve, new commitment, Born Again,
                        New beginning with God.

8. Socialization: Teach and practice survival values and
                        sound doctrines through the
                        institutions of society. Teach and
                        practice the ways of righteousness
                        social justice and freedom. Teach and
                        encourage respect for the person,
                        property, and rights of others.
                        Teach and practice reverence for God,
                        God's creation and the sacredness of
                        human life.

9. Redemption: Rising above secular, material, and
                        temporal values. Rising above
                        mundane, humanistic, and idolatrous
                        values. Reaching heights of noble
                        significance and eternal merits.

10. Transcendence: A power that goes beyond and exceeds
                        the natural powers of the world. It is the
                        ultimate omnipotent power from
                        above. A power beyond creation
                        without limitations.

11. Educational Competence :	Keeping pace with current relevant knowledge for intelligent and wise actions.
12. Commission:	Authorized methods and strategies to carry out the mission of cultural transformation.

Legislative Priorities for a Healthy Society (Long ignored and long overdue)

1. American judicial reformation is urgently needed. Judges and lawyers must be taught a sense of justice and righteousness based on truth and sound rational judgment with acknowledgement of natural and divine laws. Judicial decisions are often arbitrary, political, ideological, and biased with no justice or relationship to reality.
2. Legislation is needed that requires public officials to be accountable to their political constituency and tax paying citizens. When public officials fail to represent their constituency or when they misrepresent them it is tantamount to political and economic fraud against the American citizens.
3. Legislative Institutional Restoration is urgently needed for the historically deprived and disadvantaged Black

American families, educational institutions, religious institutions, businesses and other Black community enterprises. Historical and continuing racial discrimination continue to take a great toll on these long suffering, sacrificial and loyal Americans. They need legislated restorative help from their own Nation. This is not just a Black American need. This is a hundred percent American restoration need.

4. Urgent legislation, monitoring and strict enforcement is needed for efficient, reasonable and just time limits for judicial and administrative investigations, litigations and dispositions in the courts and administrative hearings where Civil and Human Rights are at issue and concerned. It is not unusual for hearings and litigations of Civil and Human Rights cases to languish in the judicial systems and courts for over 6 years. Justice delayed is not only justice denied, but also additional compounded injustice by the Justice System, itself.

5. Legislation is urgently needed to insure fairness, justice and equality in government employment and personnel administration through a democratic merit system based on an objective quantifiable comprehensive monitored merit system. American citizens must not be subjected to biased, prejudicial, personal favoritism systems and administration by intimidation. Such a non-merit system contradicts democracy and negates the U.S. Constitution and makes a mockery of justice.

6. A government of justice and equality of law for its citizens requires legislation prohibiting the use of arbitrarily placing citizens names on "No Hire Lists" or Black Lists" without due process of law mandated by the U.S. Constitution. The arbitrary, subjective and prejudicial use of "No Hire Lists" is an abominable crime and violation of human and Civil Rights. It makes a mockery of justice and the U.S. Constitution. The vicious and clandestine use of unlawful "No Hire Lists" are destroying professional careers, defaming characters and destroying lives of good and productive citizens. This should not be allowed in any civilized society, especially in government administration.

7. Legislation is needed to "ban the box" designating references to past employment job terminations on applications for employment. Such references are often used arbitrarily to deny employment in a prejudicial way without knowing any information about a past termination on a previous job. Many previous job terminations were not justified or fair at all. There is an extensive movement to "ban the box" for criminal records on job applications. There is also a movement to expunge criminal records so that it will not hinder employment opportunities. Legislate "ban the box" for past job terminations.

8. Legislation is needed to enforce the teaching of Comprehensive Character Education in all public schools throughout Georgia from (K-12) kindergarten through twelfth grade. Ongoing character education is essential

for the wellbeing of students as well as the good and safety of society itself. (Refer to House Bill 605, Ga. 1999).

9. Educational legislation is urgently needed for the establishment of Accelerated Compensatory Education for the historically deprived Black American students with records of low academic achievement, poor attendance, high dropout rate and other barriers to educational achievement. Compensatory accelerated education is urgently needed to catch these children up with their peers or they will forever remain behind. Helping these historically deprived children to catch up educationally, not only helps them, but it helps the community and the Nation.

10. Legislation is needed to require for the provision of professional mental health and substance abuse personnel to provide remedial, educational, preventive, and promotional services as needed for all students from (K-12) in the public schools in the State of Georgia. There is a vast and growing need for mental health, drug abuse and addiction services in the public-school systems in Georgia and throughout the Nation.

11. Legislation is needed to require the public-school systems to publish the educational Curriculum, along with the books, authors and other educational material used in the classrooms and in the education of children from K-12. This legislation must also require that parents and the community be involved in the development of the

curriculum that is taught to their children. Most parents, residents and citizens do not know the content, rationale, values and significance of what knowledge is being taught to their children.

12. Legislation is needed to require all high schools and boards of education in Georgia to adopt Georgia Law (20-2-148). Elective course in History and Literature of the Old and New Testaments Eras. Presently, this law left the option of this elective course to the local board of education to decide. Although this is an elective course, the Atlanta Board of Education has refused to adopt it in the curriculum of Atlanta Public Schools.

Civilization's Vanguard of Truth America's Culture Crisis Dictates Truth Leadership

God's commissioned clergy must be the vanguard of truth to advance the human enterprise of civilization. Truth is the foundation for human survival and triumphant living. Truth is the reality of existence. Truth is the light that illuminates reality. Truth shows the way to the greatest values known to mankind.

Truth shows the way to life love, goodness, righteousness, justice, knowledge, wisdom, understanding, peace, beauty, freedom, and God. Truth reveals what is, what was, what will be and what ought to be. Truth is created and ordained of

God. Truth is the foundation of existence. When the truth is denied, distorted, exaggerated, confused, and misrepresented, problematic crises are precipitated in the culture. Such mishap threatens the quality and existence of life.

It is critical in this twenty first century that the clergy of God assume and assert the leadership role as the vanguard of truth. The silence and passivity of God's clergy jeopardizes humanity and imperils civilization. The clergy must position itself on the front line of the ideological battle.

The clergy, individually and collectively, must be the prophetic voice of God and the resurrected witnesses of Jesus Christ. The clergy must get involved and engaged in the raging ideological spiritual warfare, which threatens human existence. The clergy must not only take a stand for righteousness and social justice; it must also take a position against evil and injustice. It must also warn the wicked of the destructive consequences of their evil.

You, who believe in God, must proclaim with urgency, the gospel truth as never before. You must put the spot light on wickedness, corruption, and perversions. You must challenge misguidance, misrepresentation, criminality, and immoralities.

The clergy vanguard for humanity must rise above partisanism, sectarianism, cultism, egotism, racism and materialism. It must be biblically based in the Word of God and theologically guided by the wisdom of God.

THIS CLERGY VANGUARD MUST HAVE A UNIVERSAL MISSION OF SPIRITUAL REDEMPTION. IT MUST HAVE A PLAN OF SOCIAL JUSTICE AND SOCIAL SALVATION.IT MUST HAVE A METHODOLOGY OF HUMAN RESTORATION. IT MUST HAVE A VISION OF PEACE AND PROSPERITY. IT MUST CULTIVATE A NEIGHBORHOOD OF BROTHERHOOD. THIS CLERGY VANGUARD MUST MANDATE A WORLD OF CIVILITY AND HUMANITY THAT GLORIFIES GOD.

The Relevant Role of Ministry in the 21st Century CAPT, Inc.
What's Going on in the American Society?

In the broad daylight of the 21st century, the local, state, and national government policy makers are ignoring the Bible in their administrative, executive, judicial and legislative practices. The diverse laws of God are being ignored. The natural laws of the Creator are being ignored. The statutory laws of the U.S. Constitution are being ignored. These respective public officials are making their own laws-but not according to righteousness, justice, and truth.

God's people are being misled by the dark arbitrary, tyrannical law of worldly secularism. Alien ideological politicians and atheistic judges are using their judicial discretion to make laws without regard to justice, righteousness, and truth. Justice ignored and justice delayed is justice denied. If America has moved into a post Biblical and post U.S. Constitution era, why have not the people been informed? Laws that are not sanctioned by divine authority, natural law or the U.S. Constitutional law are not validated laws. If such is the case, the American Judicial System is legitimizing injustice by human subjectivity and personal bias.

Questions for Clergy and Church

Is God calling only political lawyers, peanut farmers, actors, military leaders or billionaires to lead America; or is God also calling theologians and pastors to lead God's people? Why are ministers and theologians relegated to pasturing churches, teaching at seminary, officiating at weddings, funerals and other sacramental services? What responsibilities do ministers have for the general, national and global welfare? Are theologians and ministers trained by their educational institutions for the general, national and global welfare?

An Invitation for Clergy and the Church

Come from under the veil of ignorance, fear, and confusion. Come from under the veil of lies and deceptions. Come from under the veil of foolishness and wickedness. Come from under the veil of darkness and embrace God's knowledge, wisdom and light of truth, justice, and righteousness. Come from under the bondage of self-imposed inferiority and limitations.

Foundational Truths for Clergy Leadership Human Life is God's Greatest Gift to Humanity

Human life is God's most precious, sacred, and valuable gift to mankind. Human life is that creation of God that bears the image of God. God shows favoritism to mankind. Biblical Reference: "So God created man in his own image, in the image of God created he him; male and female created he them (Genesis 1:27)."

God's Initial Commandments are Relevant and Vital

The commandments that God gave to the first man and the first woman have continuing relevance for each generation upon the face of the earth. The violation of these commandments are detrimental to human life. Biblical Reference: "And God blessed them, and God said unto them, BE FRUITFUL, and MULTIPLY, and REPLENISH the EARTH, and SUBDUE IT: and have DOMINION OVER THE FISH OF THE SEA, and OVER THE FOWL OF THE AIR, and

OVER EVERY LIVING THING that moves upon the earth (Genesis 1:28)."

The Earth Belongs to God

Mankind inhabits the earth by the grace, generosity, and mercy of God. The earth provides mankind with all of the essentials for human life. God has given mankind the position of stewardship over the resources of the earth. The earth is a perpetual source and resource for the sustenance of human life. Man is a transitory tenant of the earth and not a permanent owner. It is time for man to seriously reassess his sacred responsibility as steward of the earth. Has the supervision, management, administration, accountability, and leadership been acceptable? Biblical Reference: "The earth is the LORD's and the fullness thereof, the world and they that dwell therein (Psalm 24:1)."

Social Justice Is A Human Right

Social (human) justice is the God given methodology of cultivating, distributing, and consuming the resources, values and services of the earth through the equitable administration of justice according to the righteousness, mercy and will of God. God has elevated justice as a foremost priority in governing the relationships among human beings. Justice is a balance of the scales of human rights. It is an equitable sharing of what is rightfully due to each individual based on divine law and the righteousness of God. Biblical references to justice is replete in the Bible. Proverbs 11:1, describes justice most succinctly, "A false balance is abomination to the Lord: but a just weight is his delight." When the requirement of justice is not met, there are detrimental consequences for injustice. Injustice creates a deficit in the human potential. Injustice is an act of violence. Humanity cannot continue to absorb these deficits without cataclysmic consequences. When humans fail to do justly and fail to be worthy stewards of the earth and its resources, the possibilities for human life are significantly diminished.

Some Things We Must Know About Our Children's Education

The Christian Institute of Public Theology

Preface

The proper education of children and youth is more critical and challenging than ever before in the history of America. This is especially true for the most vulnerable children, who happen to be Black, lower socio-economic status and in the urban city schools. The Brown vs. Board of Education's landmark decision of May 17,1954 has not worked well for Black children's education. The moderate desegregation that was achieved under the law, has reverted to resegregation. However, the primary problem at the turn of the 21st Century is the political and corporate takeover of public education to transform it into a predatory educational industrial complex for political control and monetary profit. The National greed for this multi-billion-dollar industry has engendered political and corporate corruption at an unparalleled magnitude. The focus has shifted from a quality public education for all children and youth to legislation creating charter schools, privatized schools, and special interests schools at taxpayers' expense. This process is seriously compromising the quality, standards, and the existence of public schools. This educational crisis may manifest itself more visibly among the Black and the poor, but the genocidal nature of this crisis is a significant threat to America. The Concerned Black Clergy, parents, the Church and other religious and educational institutions must get actively and redemptively involved TODAY, to save our children, ourselves and our Nation.

Some Things We Must Know About Our Children's Education

1. Does the educational administrative leadership reflect the parental core values and spiritual belief system? What is the educational ideology and religious faith of the school educational leadership?
2. Are the educational administrative leaders appropriately competent, morally, ethically, and

professionally fit for public school educational leadership?

3. What are the personal values (Guiding philosophical principles) and spiritual identity (Name of core religious beliefs) held or embraced by the administrative leaders and teachers of the community children?

4. Is the school environment sufficiently safe and secure for the children's physical, mental, emotional, social development, growth and spiritual wellbeing?

5. What is the complete educational content of the schools' educational curriculum? Is this educational curriculum publicly published and available for public review?

6. What are the titles and content of all textbooks, along with the names and resumes of the respective authors. What are educational goals and objectives of the educational experiences, from kindergarten through twelfth grade at the respective schools?

7. What references are used to teach students the core values of America and the significance of Black African American History? What references are used to show the significant experiences and contributions of the Black Americans?

8. How is the educational school curriculum designed to provide student proficiency in the basic knowledge of science, art, law (jurisprudence), biblical, historical and ethical knowledge?

9. How is the school curriculum designed for students to achieve functional literacy in communicating intelligently, in reading, writing, typing, speaking and through instrumental scientific technology? (computers, smart phones and other social media, etc.)

10. How is the school curriculum designed to equip students with basic vocational, para- professional, pre-college marketable job skills, especially during the middle and high school years?

11. Has this Educational District adopted the Georgia Law (O.C.G.A. 20-148,2007), the Elective Courses of the Old and New Testaments Eras as History and Literature? Please explain why or why not?

12. Does this School System teach from k-12, the Comprehensive Character Education as mandated by House Bill 605 (April 23, 1999), signed into law by Georgia Governor Roy Barnes? Please explain why or why not?

The above are some things we need to know about our children's education. We must now get busy to find out what we do not know, and insist that everything that should be done-IS DONE!

The Christian Institute of Public Theology, Inc.

The Custodians of Salvation Values

(The Christian Institute of Public Theology)

The Church and the clergy are the custodians of salvation values. Salvation values are the ethical, moral and spiritual knowledge, principals and guides that assure the holistic health and wellbeing of the people of God. Salvation values consist of the whole gospel for the whole person for the whole world.

Salvation values are designed to save human lives and souls from demise, destruction, and death. Salvation values provide systems, methods, and actions to overcome the obstacles and enemies to human life. These salvation systems, methods and actions are prescribed in the revelatory message of God in the Bible. The knowledge and message of the Bible reveal salvation values that optimize the significance, quality, and duration of human life.

The Bible is the most unique authoritative literary source regarding human salvation values. These salvation values developed, evolved and grew to fruition as contained in the Biblical history of Israel. It records the past beginnings in the Book of Genesis, the present time of human existence through Prophecy and the future eschatology in Revelations. The salvation values as recorded in the Bible consist of truth, obedience, justice, righteousness, repentance, mercy, faith, hope, love, goodness, beauty, judgment, restoration, resurrection, and redemption. The efficacy and validity of these salvation values are not only stated in the Bible, but they are also documented and demonstrated truths on living stage of human history. They have been tested in the matrix of human nature and the empirical experiences of human life. These salvation values remain salvation values (God's Word) are so reliable and real, that before they fail, "Heaven and earth will pass away."

The Church of Christ and the clergy of God must be the persistent and diligent witnesses; the uncompromising prophetic voice; and the watchful devoted custodians of the God given salvation values for the children of God.

Christian Association of Public Theologians

The following legislative and administrative recommendations will serve the cause of justice, peace, goodwill, health and prosperity in our government and society. It will enhance trust and confidence in the government and create an atmosphere of respect and hope for the future.

Recommendations:

1. PUBLIC OFFICIAL ACCOUNTABILITY - Adopt legislation requiring all public officials, local, state and federal, to provide quarterly constituent meetings

and quarterly written political updates to be made available to constituent communities.

2. FIT FOR DUTY STANDARDS - Adopt legislation requiring a minimum standard of educational, ethical, citizenship and patriotic competence for all public officials, compatible with the laws of the U.S. Constitution.

3. BIBLICAL LITERACY AND THEOLOGICAL COMPETENCE - Adopt legislation requiring Biblical literacy and theological competence courses in the curriculum of all law schools Statutory laws cannot ignore divine laws and natural laws of God and be valid in the administration of human and social justice.

4. BIBLICALJUDEO-CHRISTIAN EDUCATION- Adopt legislation requiring courses of the Old Testament and the New Testament to be taught as history and literature in all public schools. Based on theological studies (which are scientific and objective), the Judeo-Christian Bible has been validated by history to be inclusive (but not coercive) of all people. It has been validated by rigorous scholarship to be progressively revelatory, historical, redemptive, comprehensive, wholistic, universal and foundational for democratic, ethical, moral and spiritual values that are compatible with the disciplines of human nature, law, art, science and religion.

5. THEOLOGICAL REPRESENTATION IN PUBLIC POLICY - The Church and the faith community must insist on credible theological representation at the local, state and federal levels in regards to the formulation and implementation of public policy for the American people. It is dangerous for the Nation to make decisions for the people without being theologically informed.

6. ESTABLISH IMPARTIAL GOVERNMENT MERIT SYSTEMS - Establish through legislation impartial merit systems with explicit fair employment policies, practices and procedures Government must set the example for fairness and justice in its employment practices and contractual agreements and transactions involving the rights of citizens and the equitable allocation of taxpayers money. The subversion of fairness undermines trust in government. True merit systems reinforce trust in government and democracy and contributes to peace and goodwill.

7. PERSONAL LIABILITIES FOR RIGHTS VIOLATIONS - Institute legislation for personal liability for any government employee or government agent in the course of their employment, who violate the Civil Rights of a subordinate or another employee during the course of their employment with the respective agency. This

prohibits the violating employee from claiming administrative immunity from prosecution.

8. EMPLOYMENT GRIEVANCE PROCEDURE-Institute legislation requiring a fair clear and understandable grievance policy and procedure that complies with the due process of law contained in the 14th Amendment with reasonable time limits for resolution not to exceed 180 days.

9. PROHIBIT NO HIRE LISTS - Institute legislation that prohibits any government or private agency from placing the name of an employee, former employee or prospective employee on a designated no hire list without the due process of law. In the event a person's name is placed on a no hire list, after a due process hearing has been granted, specify the full nature of the no hire list, including its jurisdiction, effects, duration, removal and appeal procedure.

10. CONFLICT OF INTEREST DISCLOSURE - Institute legislation that requires legal penalties for an attorney or other legal representative to agree to represent a client for consideration and fail to disclose a known conflict of interest when entering into the contractual agreement with the client or failed to make disclosure subsequent to the agreement.

11. CIVIL RIGHT SEMINARS - It is recommended that human rights and Civil Rights seminars be held in each government agency on a monthly basis at a

convenient time and place to keep employees and citizens informed of the laws and the education about the Civil Rights of U.S. Citizens. Such meetings are also recommended for the Church and other faith organizations.

12. PROFESSIONAL CODE OF ETHICS - It is recommended that each government employee be required to subscribe to a designated code of professional ethics with explicit required conduct and behavior. Each employee is entitled to know with specificity what conduct, mannerism and expectations are required of them. It is recommended that professional codes of ethics be instituted in all agencies where people are served, including the clergy and faith-based organizations.

Proposal for Providing Character Education For Students of Private and Public Schools in Georgia

The character education described in this proposal is based on the Character Education Program that was signed into Georgia law by Governor Roy Barnes on April 23, 1999. The Law mandated that all schools in Georgia from K-12 to incorporate character education into the school educational curriculum. The components of this Character Education Law includes 27 specific enumerated character Traits as follows: cheerfulness, citizenship, compassion, cleanliness, cooperation, courtesy, courage, creativity, diligence, fairness, generosity, honesty, kindness, loyalty, patriotism, patience, perseverance, punctuality, respect for the Creator, respect for others, respect for environment, self-respect, self-control, sportsmanship, school pride, temperance, tolerance.

These character traits are designed to assist, teach, motivate and inspire students, in a comprehensive way, to develop positive attitudes, responsible behavior, ethical principles, ethical practice, successful identities, academic achievement, cultural and enrichment, personal health, peace and goodwill toward others as patriotic American citizens. These character traits will help the students to focus on the seriousness of educational achievement, the sacredness of life, the optimum use of time, personal development, moral and spiritual growth. The students will have the opportunity to learn about the great values of freedom, justice and equality that moved civilization toward peace, prosperity and democratic self-governing community living. These character traits are designed to help the students to develop autonomous self-governing and individual responsibility for personal behavior determined voluntarily internally as opposed to outside eternal involuntary enforcement. It is the expectation and hope that this character education experience will help the students to get more seriously on the time-tested validated tracks of successful living through true science, true art, true law and true religion.

This proposal is to be accomplished through trained volunteers with valid certifications to provide the above services in conjunction with the respective schools according to the guidelines, policies and procedures of the respective school. These services are to be provided to a selected number of the students (between six to twelve students) in a suitable space at the school for one-hour sessions, for once or twice each week. One or two qualified volunteers from the Faith Based Organization will lead the Character Education Group. The finalized agreement will be worked out with the designated persons from the Faith Based Organization and the Respective School where the educational and group service is to be provided.

Fundamental Traits for Character Education

The Consistent practice of the following Character traits enhances Career success in life. (Georgia Law 20-2-145)

1. Cheerfulness — Be pleasant and encouraging.
2. Citizenship — Be a responsible member of society.
3. Compassion — Develop a caring & positive concern for others.
4. Cleanliness — Practice personal & environmental cleanliness
5. Cooperation — Learn and Practice teamwork with others.

6. Courtesy — Extend friendliness & hospitality to others.

7. Courage — Be brave. Take a stand for the right thing.

8. Creativity — Use your intelligence to think/make new things.

9. Diligence — Don't give up. Hold on. Endure to the end.

10. Fairness — Treat all with respect. Give everyone their dues

11. Generosity — Develop a spirit of giving and Sharing

12. Honesty — Be real. Bonafide, Sincere, True

13. Kindness — Be pleasant, affirming, helpful and positive

14. Loyalty — Be reliable, dependable, committed.

15. Patriotism — Express care & concern for your country nation

16. Patience & Virtue — Wait with hope & endurance.

17. Perseverance — Work and struggle until success is achieved.

18. Punctuality — Be on time or ahead of time

19. Respect for the Creator — Reverence for God of the universe.

20. Respect for others — Human life & human right rights are sacred.

21. Respect for environment	Keep clean, safe & healthy.
22. Self-Respect	Keep your integrity. Be the best you can be.
23. Self-Control	Let wisdom/knowledge/ responsibility guide you
24. Sportsmanship	Play fairly. Lose gracefully. You are a winner.
25. School pride	Help your school achieve its goal by achieving yours.
26. Temperance	Keep your mind, emotions & actions balanced w/ reality.
27. Tolerance	Be understanding & Considerate of those who do not meet your expectations

The above character traits were abstracted from Georgia Law 20-2-145 and adapted by Foundation Baptist Church, Inc. to be used to teach character education in schools and other educational and human services facilities.

Foundations of Cultural Transformation
The Creator, God, Owns Everything

The earth is not owned by any person, race, religious group, nationality, or any designated people. Psalm 24:1 is explicit about the ownership of the earth and everything else. "THE EARTH IS THE LORD'S, AND THE FULNESS THEREOF;

THE WORLD, AND THEY THAT DWELL THEREIN." (Psalm 24:1). It is a tragic sadness that there are human beings who think that they have the right or the authority to, "wipe," certain other human beings off the face of the earth or otherwise use, deprive and destroy them. The reprobate minds that think this way are sick with sin, the earth and the wonderful blessings that God has created for mankind. Jesus Christ declared that he came to give life, and to give it more abundantly. The anti-Christ spirits and the anti-God spirits are determined to destroy human life and the goodness of the creation of God. The love, the resurrection, the grace and ascension of Jesus is a declaration that evil will not succeed. Every human being needs Jesus Christ as their Lord and Savior.

The Righteousness of God Is the Standard

God has already set the standards for his righteousness for all mankind. It is perilous and dangerous to substitute the righteousness of man for the righteousness of God. Therefore, it is a primary responsibility for every person to learn the righteousness of God standards as set by God. This is vitally important because Proverbs 14:12 says, "There is a way which seemeth right unto a man, but the end thereof are the ways of death." Romans10:2-3 confirms what Proverbs says in the following words, "For I bear them record that they have a zeal of God, but not according to knowledge. For they are being ignorant of God's righteousness, and going about to establish their own righteousness, have not submitted themselves unto the righteousness of God." Religious and political zeal without the righteousness of God and without the knowledge of God's Word, is perilous, deceptive, and destructive. When people deviate from the ways of God, like sheep without a shepherd, they go astray. Judges 21:25 gives insight into self-righteousness in the following verse, "In those days there was no king in Israel: every man did that which was right in his own eyes." Thanks be to God for giving humanity a righteous king in Jesus Christ. Follow King Jesus, the Christ.

The World's Most Valuable Knowledge

The most valuable knowledge in the history of mankind is the knowledge about God. The Bible is God's Special Knowledge of Revelation to Mankind. Underneath, the Bible is man's search for God. From above, it is God's revelation and self-disclosure to mankind. The Bible is knowledge about the ultimate purpose of human existence. The Bible is the Book of Truth, knowledge, Wisdom, Righteousness, Justice, Mercy, Hope, Faith, Goodness, Forgiveness, Freedom, Healing, Grace, Law, Peace, Love, Restoration, Redemption, Salvation, Light and Life. The Bible is the Book of God's Ways, Will and WORD Made Flesh in the Savior, JESUS CHRIST. The Bible is Divine, Transcendent and Spiritual Know-Ledge. This Spiritual Knowledge from God can be used through Faith to enable and empower the believer to overcome the tragic predicament of sin, suffering and death. The Bible is the true story of God's visitation into the history of mankind to deliver God's Message of Love and God's Son of Salvation. God's Message is to every soul, including You. Join Foundation in establishing more individual, home, school, work, and other community Bible Study Groups.

Focusing on Majors and Priorities

When your leadership is in crisis and your society is in confusion, it is a time to major in top priorities. Challenges for the people of God have never been more serious than they are presently, in this 21st Century. Lostness, darkness and ignorance are rampant in our society. However, there is good news in the Word of God to help us to get back on course of righteousness. There is good news in the Word of God to help us focus on what is important and what our majors and priorities should be. Joshua 24:15 says, "Choose you this day whom you will serve." Jesus says in Matthew 6:33, "But seek you first the kingdom of God, and his righteousness, and all these things shall be added unto you." Seeking the Kingdom first will cause other priorities to find their rightful place. Let us set our focus on double and triple majors and let us teach our children to do the same. Let us major in the following priorities: Knowledge, Wisdom, Understanding, Love, Justice, Peace, Righteousness, Goodness, joy and beauty.

God's Two Great Commandments to Man

God's two Great Commandments must direct our religious priorities. They can help us to establish what is most significant in life. God's Commandments direct our focus, concentration, and guidance. God's Commandments order our minds, spirits, feet and hands. They transform our hearts into love, our speech to kindness and our intentions to goodwill and peace. God's two Great Commandments direct us to the most significant values. The most important two values are life and love. God is love. God shares his love with mankind. Without love and life, other values have no significant meaning. Jesus confirms these two Great Commandments in Matthews 22:37-39 when he says," "THOU SHALL LOVE THE LORD THY GOD WITH ALL THY HEART AND WITH ALL THY SOUL, AND WITH ALL THY MIND.... THOU SHALL LOVE THY NEIGHBOR AS THYSELF." These two commandments are so basic that Jesus said that all the law and the prophets hang on them. It must be emphasized that the two Great Commandments is about loving God above and mankind below. It is not about loving material things. It is about loving life in God and loving life in mankind.

Christian Education for the Public Good

We must encourage the incorporation of Biblical knowledge, character education, civil and ethical learning in our public and private education systems for the public good. Christian education is that education that undergirds and supports all other legitimate and valid education in the Church and community. We are doing great harm to our children and Nation by not requiring Christian education in our school systems. Christian education provides the proper ethical and moral guidance and equitable regulation of all other values and services in the society. Christianity is the guiding and enlightening force for the safe and constructive use of technology in a civilized and humane society. Christianity is universal and inclusive of all people. Jesus Christ is the only universal Savior of the world. How can anyone justify the deprivation of the Good News of Jesus Christ, who is life, truth and the way?

How to Know God's Will

God's Will is knowable. God has revealed his Will. God has Revealed God's Will in the natural ordered creation. God has revealed God's Will in Biblical Divine Revelations. God has revealed God's will in Jesus Christ. In studying the handbook of God's creation, you can learn something about the Will of God. In studying God's World In the Old Testament and in the

New Testament God reveals God's Will. In accepting Jesus Christ as your Lord and Savior you can know the Will of God. Jesus Christ is the undeviating Will of God to reach mankind. It is critically important to know God's Will because your life is somewhere in the Will of God. When you learn about God's Will, you are in a better position to know God's Will for your life. It is tragic for the blindness of your will to be contrary to the will of God. When David learned he was outside the Will of God, he asked God to, "Create in me a clean heart, O God; and renew a right spirit within me." Psalms 51:10. The Bible makes over 870 references to the heart. When God cleans your heart, you will know God's Will.

Thanks Be to God

Thank you God for everything. Thank God for his excellent Creation. Thank God that he was fit to include you and me in his excellent creation. God created everything from nothing. He created you and me from nothing. God created you and me as beings who can recognize existence and see his handiwork in his marvelous creation. Why thank God? In addition to creating us from nothing with eyes, ears minds and spirits to behold his creation, God made us special. He created us in his own image and likeness. There is something about human beings that is like God. Thanks be to God. He gave us the ability to be fruitful and multiply, replenish the earth and subdue it; and to have dominion over the fish of sea, the fowl of the air and every creature that moves upon the earth. Why thank God? God has crowned humanity and with glory and honor. He has made us new creatures in Jesus Christ. God has accepted us in his Household of Faith. O'Lord, our Lord, how excellent is thy name in all the Earth!

The Need for Inward Transformation

The great and urgent need of this 21st Century is spiritual transformation within. Restricting the possession of guns, hiring more police and incarceration of more people will not make a safer society within itself. WE NEED INTERNALIZED SALVATION KNOWLEDGE. We need wisdom and understanding. We need to know the truth, the way and the life. We need a joyful, grateful and clean heart. We need a right spirit and a renewed mind. We need the mind of Christ. We need to become new creatures in Christ to transform our lives from within. This will enable us to do good, love mercy, walk humbly. This internal new life in Christ will give us goodwill and peace within in order to have peace on earth.

Believe on Jesus Today

Every person needs the Savior. Many people search for salvation through religion, church, government, various shrines, ideologies, philosophies, and doctrines. Some religions and ideologies have positive benefits and helpful services for human life and society. However, the research shows clearly that there is no salvation in any religion or other manmade institution. Salvation is found only in God through Jesus Christ. History has not revealed another resurrected savior other than Jesus Christ. Jesus is well documented in history and the Scripture as being the Savior of the world (John 3:16). It is explicitly stated in Acts: " NEITHER IS THEIR SALVATION IN ANY OTHER; FOR THERE IS NONE OTHER NAME UNDER HEAVEN GIVEN AMONG MEN, WHEREBY WE MUST BE SAVED." (Acts 4:12)

Whoever you are, believe on the Lord Jesus Christ today. Tomorrow may be too late. "How shall we escape, if we neglect so great salvation." (Hebrews 2:3) (Pastor W.J Webb)

The Purpose of Life is Love

God designed mankind for love. When we as a people fail or refuse to love, we defeat the very purpose of life. We were born because of love. We were born out of Love. We were loved before we knew ourselves. We were cared for and nurtured before we could care for ourselves. We were surrounded by love before we knew of our own existence. Our love is a response to our having been loved. Our love is a return of love that we received before we were born. We love God because he first loved us. God's love and our parents' love obligate us to love God and man. Loving God and man are intertwined. You cannot truthfully say that you love God and hate your brother or sister. God requires that we love God and our neighbor.

What is a True Religion?

A true religion is based on sound and true doctrines and practices that point to, and connect with, the will and reality of God. In true religion, God is recognized as being omnipotent, omniscient, omnipresent, infinite, eternal, immortal and Creator. The doctrines, principles, and practice of true religion must be congruent and in harmony with the following universal values: LIFE, TRUTH, JUSTICE, GOODNESS, RIGHTEOUSNESS, LOVE, LIGHT, BEAUTY, FAITH AND HOPE. True religion is universally inclusive of all human beings as brothers and sisters under the Fatherhood of God. In true religion God is worshipped in truth and in spirit. True religion allows for the autonomy of the individuals free will as opposed to coercive intimidations of the mind and the involuntary servitude of the body. True religion contains redemptive revelations from God that are specifically manifested in a historical context of invincible evidence and infallible proof. Remember that religions, prophets, doctrines, and principles can be false. Therefore, it is vitally important for everyone to seek, ask, pray and study until you have found TRUE RELIGION THAT OFFERS SALVATION IN JESUS CHRIST.

Major in Character Education

The American educational system, and especially the public schools, must begin to major in character education to save our youth and the Nation. Character education is the teaching and the transmission of the universal core moral, ethical and spiritual values for the benefit of humanity and for the common good of society. Character education teaches reverence for God, the Creator, and respect for the sacredness and dignity of human Life. The objective of character education is to instill into human personalities, validated sound core values of justice, righteousness and compassion for human life, civilized society and enriched culture. There are growing secular influences in America and throughout the world that are discouraging the cultivation of moral, ethical and spiritual values. Sinister efforts are operating to eliminate the Bible, Jesus Christ and God from society. This trend of darkness must be resisted and defeated.

The State of Georgia passed a law House Bill 605) on April 23, 1999, mandating local boards of education to implement comprehensive Character Education Programs for levels kindergarten through twelve to begin the 2000 - 2001 school year. The law required the development of the following character traits: others, kindness, cooperation, self - respect, courtesy, compassion, tolerance, diligence, generosity, punctuality, creativity, sportsmanship, loyalty, perseverance, cleanliness, cheerfulness, school pride, respect for environment, respect for creator, self-control, patience and virtue. (THIS LAW MUST BE ENFORCED!)

Character Education Transforms Culture

PARENTS with good character will teach their children the highest and most noble values for success. MEMBERS OF FAMILIES with good character will love, respect, and enhance family members for unity. TEACHERS with good character will transmit to their students true knowledge, humane and survival values. An EDUCATOR with good character, plants truth, knowledge, wisdom and sound doctrines into the learners, institutions, society, and culture. The ARTIST with good character will create, express, and spread elevated thoughts of beauty and goodness into the minds, hearts and culture of the people of God. The SCIENTIST with good character will invent methods and instruments to help human life and advance civilization. The LAWYER with good character will not compromise truth or justice or go against God's divine laws. The MINISTER with good character will teach, preach, witness, share the good news of God in Christ and be a member of the vanguard of truth for the good civilization. The LEADERS of men and nations must be led by the undeviating will of God found in the Character of Jesus Christ.

Public Theology for the World

Public theology is an objective, knowledge, wisdom and spiritual guide for the use of the gifts and resources of God. Public theology acknowledges the total sovereignty, power and authority of God. Theology acknowledges the omnipotence, omniscience, and the omnipresence of God. God has absolute jurisdiction over his creation and the affairs of mankind. There are no off limits to God. Man cannot exclude God. Man cannot get away from the presence of God. It is infantile and ludicrous for man to think that he can exclude God or escape from the presence of God. God favors man. God created man and woman in his own image. God gave man dominion over all other creatures. God gave man divine and natural law; with art, science and religion, to overcome problems and to build God's Kingdom of justice, righteousness, goodness, mercy, beauty and love upon the earth. It is the will of God for man to use these gifts to overcome the forces of evil upon the earth through Jesus Christ.

CHAPTER 13

Actualizing Life's Potentials

God created man in his own image, in the image of God created he him; Male and female created he them. And God blessed them, and God said unto them, Be fruitful, and multiply, and replenish the earth, and subdue it: and have dominion over the fish of the sea, and over the fowl of the air, and over every living thing that move upon the earth. (Genesis 1:27-28)

But ye are a chosen generation, a royal priesthood, an holy nation, a peculiar people; that ye should shew forth the praises of him who has called you out of darkness into his marvelous light. (1 Peter 2:9)

But as many as received him, to them gave he poser to become the sons Of God, even to them that believe on his name. (John 1:12)

I can do all things through Christ which strengthens me. (Philippians 4:13)

Now, therefore ye are no more strangers and foreigners, but fellow citizens with the saints, and of the household of God. (Ephesians 2:19)

Actualizing Life's Potential

The human goal is to actualize the gifts of God. It is the duty of parents, educational and developmental institutions to realize and actualize the talents, special gifts and the human potential given by God.

The development of individual potentials are to be transformed into actualizing the group corporate potentials.

This actualization process is a positive, focused, and productive process. It is progressive and developmental and allows minimum time for negativity. The process of self-actualization, generate social processes of cooperation, accommodation, and assimilation. Self and corporate actualization create unity and teamwork. A unified teamwork effort increases production and boosts morale. It amounts to mental, emotional, and spiritual empowerment.

It seems that God has created and built into man, man's salvation through self-actualization. There is deliverance and fulfillment in developing and actualizing the talents and gifts of God. Proverbs 18:16 say, "A man's gift make room for him, and brings him before great men."

Faith is a key component in self-help and accomplishing goals. James 2:26 says, 'As the body without the spirit is dead, so faith without works is dead also." To get things done requires initiatives and actions. Self-actualization requires work. The goal of the actualized self is to bless self and others, and to glorify God. Each individual life is a gift and blessing from God.

The highest expression of civilization and humanitarianism is giving and sharing blessings with others. There have been many examples of people giving and sharing with others throughout history. Giving services and material things are good and noble. The supreme gift is to give one's life for another.

The supreme giver in history is Jesus Christ. He gave his life as a sacrifice and ransom for the salvation of all people. Jesus represents a gift from God according to the well-known Scripture, John 3:16, "For God so loved the world that he gave his only begotten Son, that whosoever believe in him should not perish, but have everlasting life."

Jesus taught a salient and significant message about the options of giving. It boils down to two options. You can save your life and lose it, or you can give your life and find it. "For whosoever will save his life shall lose it: and whosoever will lose his life for my sake shall find it (Matthew 16:25)."

Self-actualization and the exploration of adventurous exciting options allow no time, energy or resources to waste or squander. Most people have many talents, latent and untapped potentials. The development and utilization of these God given talents and potentials present such great innovative and creative opportunities to express beauty, goodness, righteousness and elevated splendor; that hatred of the heart and negativity of the mind present no temptations, desires or inclinations to indulge or to succumb to the base things of the world.

Actualization of life's potentials opens up infinite possibilities for positive thinking, spiritual elevation, emotional wellbeing and inspired visions for the future. Self-actualization is not isolated or alienated living. On the contrary, at the core of self-actualization is a burning inspirational desire to love and serve others, please and glorify God.

Actualized living has a cup that is running over with love. This vibrant energy and flame of love sheds light and inspiration to others. It spreads seeds of truth, kindness, goodwill, peace, courage, and hope. The actualization of God's gifts creates a healthy giving and sharing society. It eliminates selfishness, greed, injustice, and hatred. It creates, stimulates, and motivates, and unleashes the yearning life force within. It gets rid of oppressive inhibitions and liberates the spirit to live and love.

There is a long list of gifts in the domains of art, science, law and religion. When these gifts are matched up with human needs and the mandates of God, paradise on earth can be experienced, and a foretaste of heaven on earth can be realized.

A significant key to happiness and fulfillment is to express one's talent and gifts through the artistic abilities to the benefit of man and to the glory of God. I have watched with amusement and amazement the cooking skills of culinary artists, the carpentry and building skills of builders, the martial arts skills of boxers and gymnasts the fine art of vocalists and instrumentalists. I have observed the artistic skills of barbers and beauticians, of lecturers, teachers, and preachers.

The artists who perfect their crafts and put their hearts and souls into their art, they express what it is to live and to love and to give and to share. When humans are living and loving, they have no time, no desire, no room to hate. Hatred is incompatible with love and living and with sharing and giving.

God the Creator has endowed most (if not all) his people with unusual and special talents and gifts. Most of them are never discovered, realized, or developed. It is a tragic waste and loss.

It is not just an individual blame for this lack of individual self-actualization. It is partly corporate, bureaucratic, establishment and institutional injustice that keep too many people in poverty, struggling to survive from day to day on subsistent levels. Tragically, they are prevented from being all God created them to be. This is an ongoing human tragedy, wasted lives and blighted humanity.

The following discourses are presented to provide light for this darkness, enlightenment for the ignorance and hope for the quagmire of despair. Even in the despairing darkness and ignorance there is good news. There is the potential for a great awakening, a new birth and a renaissance of righteousness and the will to live the abundant life.

MANDATES FOR HUMAN ACTUALIZATION
Greatest Book and Supreme Law

The Word of God in the Bible supersedes the U.S. Constitution and all other manmade laws. The Bible is the Book from God to mankind that has authority and jurisdiction over all mankind in all places and to all generations in heaven and in earth. The hierarchy of Biblical administration is through Jesus Christ, the Holy Spirit, and the Church of Christ. The Church receives its orders from God, the Father, Son and Holy Ghost. Every soul is subject unto God. God's message is for every person and every nation. The people of God and the Church bow only unto God. God requires all persons and all nations to bow to God. This includes all kings, emperors, queens, presidents, supreme courts, leaders, constitutions, and manmade laws. The Bible is superior to the U.S. Constitution and other manmade laws. All human beings men and women are first and foremost creatures of God, not of the state, the nation, secular society, or any other creature. God is the sole owner of human beings. Therefore, all men and all nations are accountable to God and subject to the Supreme Laws of God, And the consequences for violations.

Measuring up to the Image of God

How wonderful it would be to be the person God intended you to be. God uses the seed of man, the body of woman and the breath of life as his laboratory to make every human soul in his image. God is our Father. We are his children. We were made for the purpose of God. God is the Creator. We are his creatures and creation. God is the Potter. We are the clay. "Mold and make us after thy way." In Christ "you are no more strangers and foreigners, but fellow citizens with the saints, and of the household of God." God has given us a mind to think, the mind of Christ, a heart to love, a life to live and a soul to be saved. "We are a chosen generation, a royal priesthood, an holy nation, a peculiar people, who have been called out of darkness into his marvelous light." "Therefore, if any man be in Christ, he is a new creature: old things are passed away; behold all things are become new." In Jesus Christ, we can measure up to the image of God in us.

Honor to All Women and Mothers

Let us resolve to use this Mother's Day Celebration to honor, support and promote the sacredness of womanhood and motherhood. When we honor and support womanhood and motherhood, we are honoring and supporting the human race and the Household of God. God took woman (Eve), out of the side of (Adam), and created one flesh of the twain. However,

God chose the woman to bear all children, the boys and the girls for all succeeding generations. When men play their God given roles seriously, of supporting, protecting, respecting, loving, honoring, and praising women, we are a much stronger, healthier, happier and purpose driven people by the Will of God. Let us resolve this day to lift up and esteem womanhood and motherhood to the high, lofty and sacred place where they belong - next to God. We must teach these lessons to our children in the home, at school or wherever they may be.

Responsible Citizens Must Do More than Vote

Unfit elected officials are misrepresenting their constituents and destroying democracy and America in the process. This gross misrepresentation and abuse of authority by public officials is happening because the voting citizens fail to hold them accountable. It is commonplace for public officials to ignore and disrespect their constituents once they get into office. Tragically, they misuse the public office to enrich themselves and do favors for their relatives, personal friends and associates. Too many elected and appointed public officials have become predatory exploiters of the people and corruptors of government. Greed and corruption have become so prevalent that government public policy is being set by economic bribery and administrative intimidation.

Government agents are using taxpayers' money and citizens resources to enrich and enhance their personal ambitions. Responsible citizens have a sacred duty to clean out the unfit greedy and corrupt politicians and replace them with ethical and competent men and women who will represent the people with righteousness, justice and benevolence. We must do more than just vote. We must put in competent, ethical and persons of integrity who believe in the sacredness of human life and the sovereignty of God.

The Urgent Priority of Education

Success in education is a top priority for every child and person. The failure to get a quality education translates into the destruction of human life. The failure of adequate education creates hopelessness and despair. Human potentials are wasted. Dreams are unborn. Investment in the future is negated. Talents and gifts of the human potential are unrealized. Humanity and civilization cannot afford this colossal failure of educational achievement. A special effort is urgently needed to make quality education a top priority for every child and person. A quality education will equip students with the essential knowledge and skills to make a positive and productive livelihood and life. A quality education will bring about: (1) HUMANE CHARACTER FORMATION, (2) HUMAN NATURE CULTIVATION, (3) TRUTH REALIZATION, (4) SPIRITUAL AWAKENING, (5) SELF ACTUALIZATION. These vital educational achievements will enable the student to hind his or her best self-identity, divine purpose in life and right relationship with mankind and God. This QUALITY EDUCATION will add to the Word: GLORY TO GOD IN THE HIGHEST, ON EARTH PEACE, GOD WILL TOWARD MEN (Luke 2:14).

Urgent Need for Black Deprived Youth: Accelerated Compensatory Education

Human beings have a human right to knowledge and education to sustain life and a livelihood to keep them from perishing. A large number of Black youth are being deprived of a quality education. Many of them are depriving themselves. Many of these youth are being inadequately educated. The deprivation of education and the means of making a livelihood is genocide. A quality education, along with the technological tools for work and a just opportunity for employment are essential for a sustainable livelihood and life, itself. The high rate of school suspensions, dropouts, educational failures, lack of economic opportunities, lack of moral and spiritual guidance, are destroying our youth and our future. Educational institutions must immediately make accelerated compensatory quality education a top priority for God's children and citizens of America. Compensatory involves the necessary supports, additional personnel, and services to concentrate and speedup the educational process for the students who are deprived and behind. The deprivation of a quality education is equivalent to the deprivation of life, itself. This urgent educational need must be considered an emergency requiring immediate attention!

What is Your Spiritual ID (Identification)?

God has given identification to those who accept him. In the beginning, God gives man (includes woman) a positive and Significant Identification by creating them in God's image (Gen 1:27). Accepting Jesus Christ as your Lord and Savior, provides you with the spiritual identification of God. Our spiritual identification with God is your most significant identification (1 John 4:1-3). When you accept Jesus Christ as Lord and Savior, you become born Again (John 3:7) and a new creature (2 Cor. 5:17) in Christ. Your spiritual identification in Christ makes you a part of a chosen generation, a royal priesthood, an holy nation and a peculiar people (1 Peter 2:9-10) called out of darkness into his marvelous light as people of God. Our spiritual identification in Christ brings us near by the blood of Christ (Ephesians 2:13). Therefore, Paul says that we are no longer aliens; we are no more strangers and foreigners, but fellow citizens with the saints, and the household of God (Ephesians 2:19). We are the children of the light and the day (Thessalonians 5:5) not of the night or the darkness. Our spiritual identification is based on our confession that Jesus is the Son of God and God dwells in him (1 John 4:15) and that God is love and he that dwells in God dwells in love (1 John 4:16).

Believe on Jesus Today

Every person needs the Savior. Many people search for salvation through religion, church government, various shrines, ideologies, philosophies, and doctrines. Some religions and ideologies have positive benefits and helpful services for human life and society. However, the research shows clearly that there is no salvation in any religion or other manmade institution. Salvation is found only in God through Jesus Christ. History has not revealed another resurrected savior other than Jesus Christ. Jesus is well documented in history and the Scripture as being the Savior of the world (John 3:16). It is explicitly stated in Acts: "NEITHER IS THEIR SALVATION IN ANY OTHER: FOR THERE IS NONE OTHER NAME UNDER HEAVEN GIVEN AMONG MEN, WHEREBY WE MUST BE SAVED." (Acts 4:12)

Whoever you are, believe on the Lord Jesus Christ today. Tomorrow may be too late. "How shall we escape, if we neglect so great salvation. (Hebrews 2:3)

Foundation Principles For Sobriety and Success

1. You are a special and unique human being. Be thankful you are special. Rejoice in your uniqueness. Use your uniqueness in creative ways to improve yourself to make a better civilized humanity.

2. You are American. Embrace your Americanism. You have birth rights in America. America is your country. It is your national home. America is a country of freedom and opportunity. Often, more often than not, these opportunities are not given to you. They are available for you. You must prepare yourself to take the advantage of the available opportunities. You must be diligent and assertive in taking the full advantage of the available opportunities. More aggressive people may even take opportunities that are available for you. These opportunities in America are up for grabs. The competition is stiff. You are an American. Work hard and be intentional in fulfilling your dreams.

3. In order to be motivated to work hard, you must choose a "Success Identity." You must identify with success, not with failure. You must choose to be a "Winner." Be a competitor. Be an overcomer. Be a fixer. Be a Survivor. Be a Champion. Be a long-distance runner. You are going to run into opposition. You are going to encounter People who do not want you to succeed. Do not give up. Hold on and hold out. Be a Good soldier. Fight the good fight. Keep the faith.

4. Choose and develop your best self. Only you can become the person that you want to be. Remember, you become what you admire; you become what you aspire to be. You have the power to choose and decide what and who you want to be. You make your own

decisions. Choose wisely. Human nature is flexible. It is like wet clay. It can be shaped and formed in a variety of ways. It is your decision. Only your decision to choose to be the best person and the best self that you can will count towards who you become.

5. Invest in the future. Prepare and plan for future success. Don't gamble with your future. Set lofty goals. Work hard and work smart to reach those goals. The mark of a high-class person is that they are oriented toward the future. They don't live just for today. They invest in the future.

6. Be aware of the new and developing technology. Technology can be used for good or bad. It can be used to make life better or worse. These cell phones are handy, but they can also be disruptive. There is even talk of putting microchips under the skin to track or reveal certain information about you. Be aware of DNA. Be aware of your DNA. Be aware where you leave your DNA. It can be used to help or hurt you.

7. God has revealed himself, his Will, his Way, his Wisdom, his Standards, his Works and his Love in human history. It is the responsibility of each individual to learn for himself or herself, this historical revelation of God in our history. No one else can make your God decision for you. You must decide on God for yourself.

8. There is a moral law that says, "You Reap what You Sow." Therefore, give the world the best that you have

and the best will come back to you. You get back what you send out. Send out good things. Good things will come back to you. By the same token, if you send out bad things, bad things will come back to you. Sow good seeds and you will reap good fruit.

9. To be successful you must develop a consistent and persistent work ethic. You must not waste your time. You must not sleep it away; day dream it away or play it away. You must work hard, and you must work smart. You must work to be the best.

In the words of Dr. Benjamin E. Mays, who was President of Morehouse College for 27 years: You must do your job so well, that no man living and no man dead, and no man yet to be born can do that job any better."

Public Theological Perspective

Public theology is established under the jurisdiction and the authority of God. God, the Creator, has communicated his will and ways to mankind on the planet earth through the Bible, Jesus Christ, the Holy Spirit and the majestic creation and revelations of the universe.

God has sovereign jurisdiction and authority over all creation. There are no off-limits to God. As public theologians and agents of God, God has provided four distinct domains of knowledge for mankind to carry out his Will on earth. These four primary domains of knowledge are: Science, Art, Law, and Theology (religion). They are designed to be used for the fulfillment and actualization of their human potential and to glorify God. Science investigates, educates, manipulates, duplicates and remediates. Art creates, validates, balances, harmonizes and beautifies. The law regulates, legislates, segregates, integrates and mandates. Theology (religion) communicates, mediates, regenerates, translates, elevates and conciliates the minds, spirits and wills of God and mankind.

Public theology proclaims the whole Bible for the whole person and for the whole world under the authority of Jesus Christ and the power of God. Public theology is established upon the following Biblical foundations:

1. Biblically based in the Will of God.
2. Theologically guided by the WORD of God.
3. Existentially empowered by the ANOINTMENT of God.
4. Contextually engaged in the COMMISSION of God.
5. Prophetically proclaimed in the WITNESS of God.
6. Strategically planned through the WISDOM of God.
7. Systematically developed through the WAYS of God.
8. Holistically designed for the WORK OF God.

Public theology is not limited to theoretical knowledge or historical accounts about the Bible and religion. Public theology covers the ultimate spectrum about human life. It reveals the significance and meaning of life and how human life is designed to be lived according to the will of God.

The practice of public theology is the expansion of private religion outside of the walls and restricted confinement of the church. Public theology embraces the full mission of God on earth and in the world under the unlimited jurisdiction, power and authority of God. Public theology utilizes the blessings and salvation gifts of God in science, art, law and theology/religion for the redemption of mankind.

BIBLIOGRAPHY/REFERENCES

Alcoholics Anonymous. Living Sober. New York: World Services, Inc., 1975.

American Psychiatric Association (1994), Diagnostic and Statistical Manual of Mental Disorders (4th ed.) Washington, DC: 1994.

American Psychiatric Association. Diagnostic and Statistical Manual of Mental Disorders (5th ed.). Washington, DC: 2013. Barth, Roland S. Improving the Schools from Within. San Francisco: A Wiley Company, 1990.

Benne, Robert. The Paradoxical Vision, A Public Theology for the Twenty-First Century. Augsburg: Fortress Press, 1995.

Bettelheim, Bruno. The Informed Heart. New York: Avon Books, 1971.

Blanchard, Ken and Hodges, Phil. The Servant Leader. Nashville: Thomas Nelson, 2003.

Brick, John. Drugs, the Brain, and Behavior. New York: Harworth Medical Press, 1998.

Bright, John. A History of Israel. Philadelphia: Westminster Press, 1972.

Buttrick, George Arthur (ed.) The Interpreters Bible. New York: Abingdon Press, 1952

Clinebell, Howard. Basic Types of Pastoral Care and Counseling. Nashville, 1984.

Corey, Gerald. Theory and Practice of Counseling and Psychotherapy. Pacific Grove, CA: Brooks Cole Publishing Co., 1977.

Cone, James H. Black Theology: A Documentary History. New York: Orbis Books, 1993.

Cox, Harvey. The Secular City. New York, The MacMillan Co., 1965.

DuBois, W.E.B. Dark Water: Voices from Within the Veil. Mineola: NY: Dover Publication, 1999.

DuBois, W.E.B. The Souls of Black Folk. New York: Vintage Books, 1990.

Egan, Gerard. The Skilled Helper. Boston: Brooks/Cole Publishing Co., 1998.

Everly, George S. and Lating, Jeffrey. Psychotraumatology. New York: Plenum Press, 1995.

Felder, Cain Hope. Stony The Road We Trod. Minneapolis: Fortress Press, 1991.

Fosdick, Harry Emerson. The Modern Use of the Bible. New York: McMillan Co., 1961.

Frazier, E. Franklin. On Race Relations. Chicago: University Press, 1968.

Friere, Paulo. Pedagogy of the Oppressed. New York: Continuum Publishing Co., 1997.

Grant, Joanne. Black Protest: History, Documents, and Analyses. New York: Fawcett Premier, 1968.

Gray, Fred D. The Tuskegee Syphilis Study. Montgomery, Al. New South Books, 1998.

Hanson, Rick. Buddha's Brain. Oakland CA: New Harbinger Publications, Inc., 2009.

Hodgson, Peter C., King, Robert H., Readings in Christian Theology. Minneapolis: Fortress Press, 1985.

Hyder, O. Quentin. The Christian's Handbook of Psychiatry. Old Tappan, New Jersey, 1973.

Iorg, Jeff. Ministry in the New Marriage Culture. Nashville: Publishing Group, 2015.

James, Muriel, Jongeward, Dorothy. Born to Win. Massachusetts: Perseus Books, 1996.

Jones, James H. Bad Blood: The Tuskegee Syphilis Experiment. New York: Macmillan Publishing Company, 1981.

Mark, Veron H. Bain Power. Boston: Houghton Mifflin Co., 1989.

Masters, Kim J. The Angry Child. Santa Monica, CA: Psychiatric Hospital Division, 1993.

Montessori, Maria. The Absorbent Mind. New York: Dell Publishing, 1967.

Quarles, Benjamin. The Negro in the Making of America. New York: MacMillan Publishing Co., 1987.

Roberts, Deotis J. The Prophethood of Black Believers. Louisville, KY: Knox Press, 1994.

Simeons, A.T.W. Man's Presumptuous Brain. New York: E.P. Dutton & Co. 1962.

The Holy Bible (King James Version)

Tillman, William M. Understanding Christian Ethics. Nashville: Broadman & Holman Publishers, 1988.

Twerski, Abraham. Addictive Thinking, Center City, Minn: Hazelden, 1997.

Urschel, Harold C. Healing the Addicted Brain. Naperville, Illinois: Sourcebooks Inc., 2009.

Walker, David. David Walker's Appeal. Baltimore, Md: Black Classic Press, 1993.

Washington, Booker T. Up From Slavery. Doubleday, Page & Co., 1901.

Webb, W.J. Psychotrauma: The Human Injustice Crisis. Lima, Ohio: Fairway Press, 1990.

Webb, W.J. God's Spiritual Prescriptions.

Webb, W.J. The Way Out of Darkness.

Wright, Bobby E. Psychopathic Racial Personality. Chicago: Third World Press, 1984.

Yalom, Irvin D. The Gift of Therapy New York: Harper Collins Publishers, 2002.